INDIRA

DEVAPRIYA ROY
PRIYA KURIYAN

cntxt

First published by Context, an imprint of Westland Publications Private Limited, in 2018

Published by Context, an imprint of Westland Books, a division of Nasadiya Technologies Private Limited, in 2025

No. 269/2B, First Floor, 'Irai Arul', Vimalraj Street, Nethaji Nagar, Alapakkam Main Road, Maduravoyal, Chennai 600095

ISBN: 9789371973663

10 9 8 7 6 5 4 3 2 1

Typeset by SÜRYA, New Delhi
Cover design by Priya Kuriyan
Printed at Thomson Press (India) Ltd

This book is for Sarah Anne Cherian and Priyanka Mukherjee, a belated offering for their fourteenth and eighteenth birthdays respectively. We hope they find some of the joy we did in the story of Indira Gandhi, and that the best of Mrs Gandhi's life, her spunk, her openness to ideas and beauty, and her remarkable resilience, will enter and transform theirs.

1

IN WHICH WE MEET INDIRA THAPA

It was a regular day at school. The sun was beating down on the concrete 'play area' where no one ever played, and the two or three potted plants kept by the empty porch were wilting wistfully.

Most of the classrooms were occupied by sleepy students looking out of the windows on to the busy street outside. A few were dreaming of the iced lolly they'd buy from the man who parked himself outside the school gate every afternoon. Several dreamed of hot food (the mid-day meal at school was so boring that they would begin to imagine what their mothers might be cooking at home or at work while eating the compulsory khichdi or dal-chawal, sitting in long rows on the verandahs). The majority, though, dreamed of the summer vacation that would begin as soon as the bell rang. One whole month of no homework, no tests, and only play.

In Class VI (A), Indira Thapa, our heroine, unconcerned about silly things like summer vacations or iced lollies, was sitting on the first bench (as usual), so deep in thought over the day's assignment that five minutes had gone by without her hand flying into the air to answer a question. She had copied the words 'Oral History', which were written in gigantic letters on the blackboard, and underlined them three times for good measure. She was still not sure what they meant.

Around her, everyone was animatedly discussing the 'creative' assignment that had been set by their teacher: Write an essay around your name. Not about, around. It would be due on the Monday they returned from the holidays.

'Yes, yes,' the teacher explained, for the seventh time, widening her eyes slightly and raising herself on tiptoe, 'I want you to think about your name—given name, good name, shubh naam, whatever you call it!—find out who named you and why. Even you, Happy Jeet Singh. Don't sulk. Your name, in fact, is easier than everyone else's. Okay? Now please start packing your bags. The bell is about to ring.'

While the class chatters and Indira pores over her notebook, meet Miss Reema Das.

Light of their life and object of their obsession, Miss Das was short, bespectacled and reed-thin. Despite the cotton saree she diligently wore in a bid to look older and, more truthfully, to not be mistaken for a student, she did not look a day more than twenty-three. Which is what her age was. Unlike their regular teachers, who were tired, quasi-parental figures who barked orders and emitted a rough-and-ready sort of affection, Miss Das was—there could be no other word for it—coooooool. She was funny and unexpected and deeply interested in what the kids had to say. She brought her laptop to class on double-period days and allowed everyone to work on it by turns. And, best of all, she was surprisingly open about her life. The kids knew everything. She had studied English Lit-e-ra-ture in Lady Shri Ram College, loved mutton biriyani, lived with a roommate who was an artist, and the guy who came to pick her up in a red Nano after classes was not her boyfriend.

While Indira paid attention in every class, even in geography, where Mr Patel simply made them underline the whole chapter in the textbook day after day after day, her level of commitment to English, which Miss Das taught, was something else altogether. You see, Indira worshipped Miss Das. She waited for the bell to ring on Fridays just so she could go over to Miss Das's desk and confer urgently about things. It was her favourite time in the whole week.

As the classroom emptied, and the students fanned out boisterously in search of their iced lollies or computer games or gol gappas, Miss Das would perch on the desk and answer all of Indira's questions—her voice echoing slightly against the walls—with an amused smile. At some point the guy with the red Nano would call and, together, Miss Das and Indira would walk down to the gate where their paths would diverge. Miss Das would go to Vasant Vihar, where she lived with her friend-the-artist in a barsaati. Indira would trudge up the hill to Basant Gaon, where she lived with her mother and pet kitten, Chanda.

Today, though, Miss Das was in a bit of a hurry. Apologetically, she told Indira she would have to run to the bank. When she saw Indira's face fall, she said quickly, 'I know you wanted to discuss the assignment. Why don't you come visit me tomorrow at home? I'll WhatsApp the details to your mother. Okay?' She patted Indira on the shoulder, slightly distracted, and grabbing her bags which were bursting with answer scripts to correct, she rushed out.

Indira went back to her desk and sat down quietly.

The empty room was so peaceful. On days like this, she could pretend the large room was all her own. Now that her noisy classmates were gone, birds would come in twos and threes and peck on the sills: timid mynahs, bossy pigeons, and even a glorious parakeet or two.

Thanks to the topic of the 'creative' assignment, the meaning of her own name kept circling in Indira's head; she realized she did not know the dictionary meaning at all. From the time she was a toddler, she had known that she was named after Indira Gandhi, the lady with the bird-shaped streak of white in her hair. Once in a while, she would come across Indira Gandhi's face on a large hoarding and feel a little thrill. When she tried in her conscientious manner to lead her intractable, childish, and often utterly useless classmates towards light in some matter or another, that wretched Happy Singh or one of the others would say, 'Enh, there goes our Prime Minster', but even in her annoyance, she felt a little thrill. 'It's mi-ni-ster,' she would correct them primly. Why was she stuck in a class with such louts?

Indira sighed theatrically and picked up her bag. On the way home, through the dusty street that climbed uphill, between the abandoned park and the row of busy shops, she found a few fat dark clouds had appeared from nowhere. As a sudden wind rose, Indira had to break into a run for the last five hundred metres to avoid the rain.

Her mother, Arati, had already reached home and was hurriedly cooking them lunch. 'Why are you panting?' she asked Indira in Nepali, looking suddenly worried.

'Oh, nothing,' Indira said, and began to take off her shoes and socks. 'I ran to get out of the rain, and then climbed the stairs quickly, that's all.' Arati got Indira a glass of water.

Indira and Arati's room was the smallest they had lived in till now, and to tell you the truth, they had lived in many small rooms in the last few years. Their previous building had a nice, airy room with a separate kitchen but, unfortunately, it had caught fire one night. Not only did most of their stuff get ruined, they also had to move again. Everyone said the landlord would get a lot of insurance money, but he didn't even return their deposit. Mother, daughter and kitten had to shift again, and thanks to the timing (Arati had just sent money to her parents in Darjeeling), the only room they could afford was basically a box.

But then, Arati had magic in her fingers.

When Indira woke up in the morning to the melody of her mother's utensils, she would observe how their box was like a cozy train-ka-kamra, with the sunlight streaming on to their mattresses and pillows from the single window high up. When she returned from school, the mattresses and pillows would be hidden from sight; a table stood in their place with two chairs. These had been folded away and kept out in the corridor overnight—locked to the stairs with a chain, since not all their neighbours could be trusted. Some days, Arati would even have time to add a tablecloth before they sat down for lunch.

Afterwards, Indira would sit at the table and read one of the storybooks from Miss Das's 'mobile library' and painstakingly look up meanings of new words from the battered dictionary she had rescued from a Vasant Vihar dumpster. Arati would, meanwhile, wash clothes, make preparations for dinner, take another bath, do a second round of puja and, secretly, between comings and goings, admire Indira reading. Then, a cup of tea and a glass of milk later, one would rush to Vasant Vihar, to her job, while the other walked at a leisurely pace to her tuition.

'Ma, it's five o'clock!' Indira said. Time for both to leave. The sudden shower had left no trace bits of cloud in the sky. The sun was back, and it was as hot as ever. 'Ma,' Indira said, as Arati locked the door, an umbrella under her arm, 'I have to do some research about Indira Gandhi at the cyber café after tuition. Can you give me ten rupees?'

1966, MID JANUARY.
LONDON.
IT'S THE AGE OF ROCK 'N' ROLL!
We can work it out... We can work
Paul I Love You!
MARRY ME RINGO
CHICAGO.
A NEW REVOLUTION LED BY REVD. MARTIN LUTHER KING JR. IS CALLING FOR THE EQUALITY OF ALL RACES.
I HAVE A DREAM...
IN INDIA, FROM CALCUTTA TO KUTCH, THERE IS ONLY ONE QUESTION ON EVERYONE'S LIPS.
WHO WILL BE THE NEXT PRIME MINISTER?

EVEN AS THE SUDDEN DEMISE OF LAL BAHADUR SHASTRI, THE SECOND PRIME MINISTER OF THE COUNTRY, IS BEING MOURNED, NAMES OF POLITICIANS FLOAT ABOUT...

Y.B. CHAVAN
S.K. PATIL
GULZARILAL NANDA
SANJIVA REDDY
K. KAMARAJ
THERE ARE MANY HOPEFULS.

BUT BY 19 JANUARY, IT HAS COME DOWN TO TWO CONTENDERS: THE 70-YEAR-OLD GANDHIAN, MORARJI DESAI...
IT'S MY TURN.

AND MRS INDIRA GANDHI, THE INFORMATION AND BROADCASTING MINISTER IN SHASTRI'S CABINET AND THE ONLY DAUGHTER OF JAWAHARLAL NEHRU, INDIA'S FIRST PRIME MINISTER.
19 JANUARY AT 1 SAFDARJUNG ROAD, MRS GANDHI'S RESIDENCE.
TODAY, AT 11 A.M., THE CONGRESS PARLIAMENTARY COMMITTEE WILL ELECT ITS NEW PRIME MINISTER, BY SECRET BALLOT.

BIBIJI, GAADI TAYYAR HAI.
IT'S STILL FAIRLY EARLY IN THE MORNING, AND THE ROAD TO RAJ GHAT IS QUITE EMPTY.
AT BAPU'S SAMADHI, MRS GANDHI SITS FOR A WHILE, REMINISCING ABOUT THE PAST.

IN MANY WAYS, HER RELATIONSHIP WITH BAPU WAS FREER THAN HER FATHER'S WITH HIM. WHEN NEHRU DISAGREED WITH BAPU, IT WAS ALWAYS WITH THE RESPECTFUL DEFERENCE (AND INTENSE FRUSTRATION) OF AN INDIAN SON.
POVERTY CAN ONLY BE REMOVED THROUGH VILLAGE RE-DEVELOPMENT. WE MUST FOCUS ONLY ON THAT.
HMM... BUT POVERTY CANNOT BE REMOVED WITHOUT INDUSTRIALIZATION!
INDU, AU CONTRAIRE, DID NOT HESITATE TO SPEAK HER MIND.
EEWW! THIS IS AWFUL. HOW CAN YOU EAT IT?
HAHA. BUT GOAT CURD IS GOOD FOR YOU, INDU.
AND LATER, WHEN IT CAME TO MORE IMPORTANT THINGS...
I'VE DECIDED, BAPU. FEROZE AND I ARE GOING TO GET MARRIED. AND SOON.
IT'S OKAY THAT YOU WANT TO GET MARRIED, BUT GIVEN YOUR DUTY TO THE NATION, MAYBE YOU SHOULD CHOOSE A LIFE OF BRAHMACHARYA AFTER MARRIAGE?
WHY ON EARTH WOULD ANYONE WANT TO DO THAT?
DIFFERENCES APART, INDU LEARNT HER MOST PROFOUND LESSONS IN SATYAGRAHA FROM BAPU.
IN 1932, THE BRITISH GRANTED SEPARATE ELECTORATES TO DIFFERENT RELIGIOUS COMMUNITIES, INCLUDING THE 'UNTOUCHABLES' AS A DISTINCT MINORITY. MAHATMA GANDHI WAS THEN IN YERAWADA JAIL, AND WENT ON A FAST TO PROTEST THIS.
BAPU WAS IN FAVOUR OF RESERVATION TO THE 'DEPRESSED CLASSES' WITHIN THE HINDU ELECTORATE, BUT HE WAS CERTAIN THE 'COMMUNAL AWARD' WAS PART OF THE BRITISH STRATEGY OF DIVIDE AND RULE.
AFTER SEVERAL DAYS, DR AMBEDKAR YIELDED AND THE POONA PACT WAS SIGNED. TILL THE END OF HIS LIFE, THOUGH, HE MAINTAINED IT HAD BEEN . . .
BLACKMAIL!

THIRTEEN-YEAR-OLD INDU, THEN A RESIDENTIAL STUDENT AT THE PUPILS' OWN SCHOOL IN POONA, MADE ORANGE JUICE.
IN THE PRESENCE OF GURUDEV RABINDRANATH TAGORE, BAPU BROKE HIS FAST.
YEARS LATER, AFTER PARTITION, AS A STREAM OF BROKEN, BATTERED MEN AND WOMEN CAME TO DELHI, INDU BEGAN TO VOLUNTEER AT THE REFUGEE CAMPS.
MRS GANDHI, YOU'VE BEEN HERE SINCE LAST NIGHT... GO HOME... GET SOME REST.

ONE DAY, IN DELHI...
I WOULD LIKE YOU TO GO TO THE MUSLIM AREAS AND REPORT TO ME ON THE SITUATION THERE.
WHO WILL GO WITH ME?
IF I HAD FOUND SOMEONE TO GO, I WOULDN'T HAVE ASKED YOU... I KNOW YOU ARE UNWELL...
SHE FOLLOWED BAPU'S INSTRUCTIONS, FOUND HER WAY TO THE MUSLIM AREAS (HER DRIVER REFUSED TO GO) AND FOUND 200,000 PEOPLE LIVING IN FILTH, SQUALOR AND GREAT FEAR FOR THEIR LIVES.
SUBHADRA DATTA (LATER JOSHI) WAS HER COMRADE IN THIS MISSION...
MEANWHILE, BAPU ASSUMED THAT INDU HAD NOT BEEN ABLE TO TAKE UP THE ASSIGNMENT.
DID I NOT TELL YOU TO DO SOMETHING?
YES, AND I HAVE BEEN DOING IT.
WHY DIDN'T YOU COME BY AND TELL ME BEFORE?
BECAUSE I THOUGHT DOING IT WAS MORE IMPORTANT THAN REPORTING ON IT!

LATER IN THE DAY, MRS GANDHI GOES TO TEEN MURTI HOUSE.
TEEN MURTI, OR 'THE BIG HOUSE', HAD BEEN HER HOME FOR SIXTEEN YEARS WHEN HER FATHER WAS THE PRIME MINISTER. SHE HAD MOVED IN TO TAKE CARE OF HIS AFFAIRS, WHILE HER HUSBAND REMAINED IN LUCKNOW. IT HAD QUICKLY BECOME A HOME FOR HER BOYS, WITH ITS LARGE GROUNDS AND EXOTIC ANIMALS. FEROZE WOULD COME AND GO, BUT IT WAS NEVER A HOME FOR HIM.

FOREVER TORN BETWEEN THE NEEDS OF HER HUBAND AND FATHER, INDU CHOSE THE PECULIAR LONELINESS OF LIFE IN THE BIG HOUSE.
SHE METICULOUSLY ATTENDED TO HER FATHER'S NEEDS, BUT... A GLASS WALL WOULD SHOOT UP AROUND HIM AS SOON AS HE SAT DOWN TO WORK.
HE WAS THE PRIME MINISTER OF INDIA AND HAD BURDENS THAT NOT EVEN HIS BELOVED ONLY CHILD COULD SHARE.

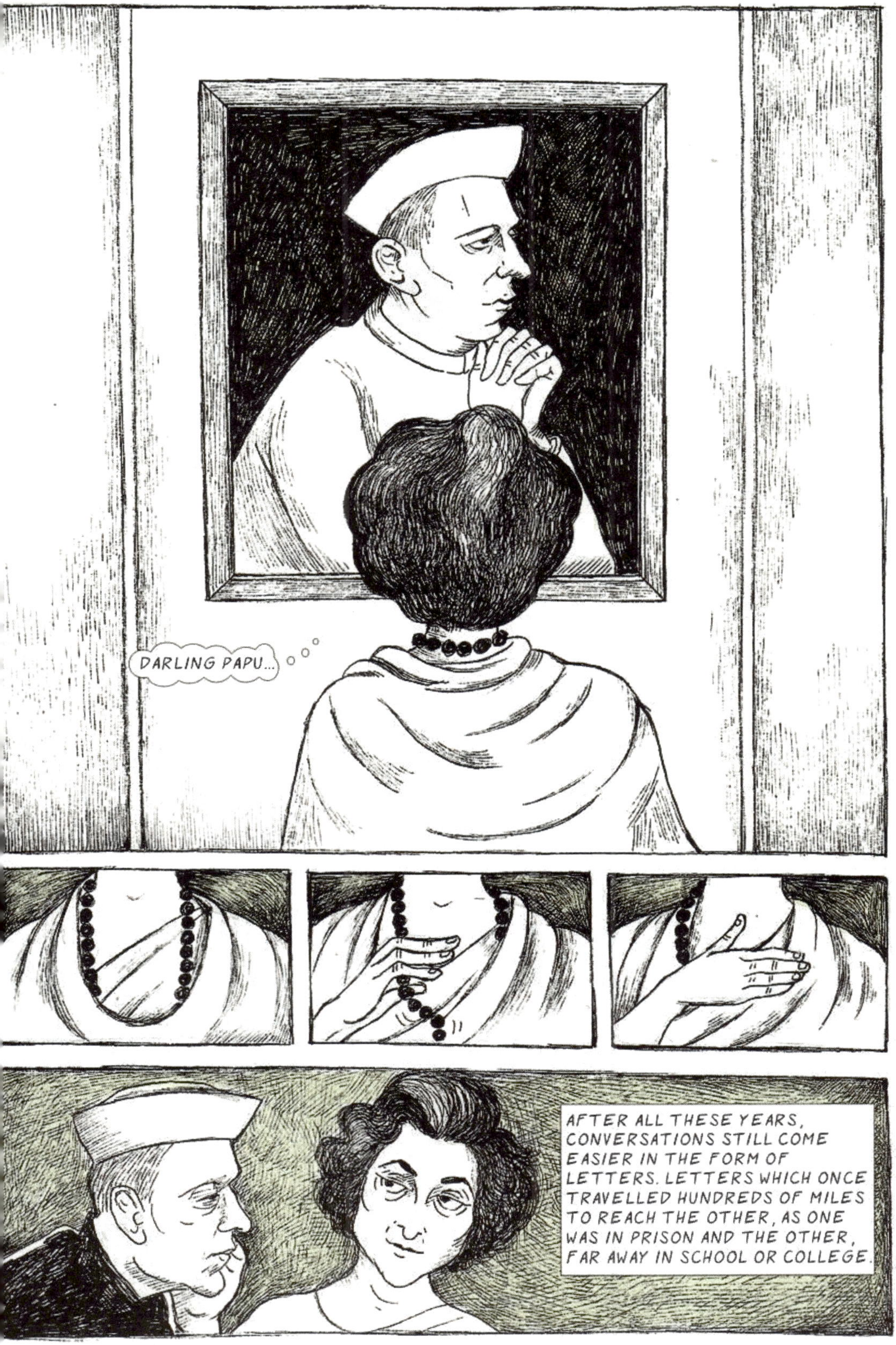
DARLING PAPU...
AFTER ALL THESE YEARS, CONVERSATIONS STILL COME EASIER IN THE FORM OF LETTERS. LETTERS WHICH ONCE TRAVELLED HUNDREDS OF MILES TO REACH THE OTHER, AS ONE WAS IN PRISON AND THE OTHER, FAR AWAY IN SCHOOL OR COLLEGE.

CAW!
TEEN MURTI HOUSE STANDS IMPASSIVE AND COLD NOW, A MUSEUM.
FROM TEEN MURTI HOUSE, ACCOMPANIED BY GULZARILAL NANDA, THE ACTING PRIME MINISTER, AND SUBHADRA JOSHI (OLD FRIEND/FRENEMY), MRS GANDHI HEADS TO PARLIAMENT HOUSE WELL BEFORE THE APPOINTED HOUR OF 11 A.M.

JUST AS SHE IS ABOUT TO ENTER, SOMEONE GIFTS HER A BOUQUET OF ROSES.
SUBHADRA JOSHI IS FOREVER ALERT TO THE MOMENT.
LAAL GULAAB ZINDABAD!
KYA BAAT HAI!

INSIDE THE CENTRAL HALL, VOTING PROGRESSES EXTREMELY SLOWLY.
TWENTY-SIX MEMBERS HAVE COME FROM VARIOUS HOSPITALS AND AT LEAST ONE MEMBER IS SO ILL, HE MUST CAST HIS VOTE FROM A WHEELCHAIR.
IF VOTING IS SLOW, COUNTING TAKES FOREVER!

FINALLY, THE CHIEF WHIP APPEARS.
LADKA HUA YA LADKI?
LADKI!
MRS GANDHI HAS WON. 355 VOTES TO 169.

WILL YOU BLESS MY SUCCESS, MORARJI BHAI?
I GIVE YOU MY BLESSING.
NEITHER OF THEM KNOWS IT, BUT THERE WILL COME A DAY WHEN MORARJI RANCHHODJI DESAI WILL REPLACE MRS GANDHI AS THE PRIME MINISTER OF INDIA, BUT THAT IS STILL MANY YEARS AWAY.

EVEN AMIDST THE JUBILATION, MRS GANDHI KNOWS THE STEELY TRUTH IN HER HEART.
THE COUNTRY IS IN THE MIDDLE OF MANY CRISES. THE MONSOONS FAILED LAST YEAR AND THERE ARE ACUTE FOOD SHORTAGES IN MANY STATES. A LANGUAGE WAR IS BREWING IN THE PUNJAB AND A SECESSIONIST MOVEMENT IN NAGALAND. THE ECONOMY IS REELING FROM INFLATION, AND FOREIGN EXCHANGE IS IN SHORT SUPPLY.
LAAL GULAAB ZINDABAD!
JAWAHARLAL KI JAI!
INDIRA KI JAI!
WORST OF ALL, SHE KNOWS, 'THE SYNDICATE' WHO SUPPORTED HER IN THE ELECTION AND RALLIED VOTES ON HER BEHALF, DID SO BECAUSE THEY THINK SHE IS YOUNG AND INEXPERIENCED, WEAK AND IMPRESSIONABLE, 'A CHIT OF A GIRL'. THEY IMAGINE THEY CAN IMPOSE THEIR WAYS AND VIEWS UPON HER, AND RUN HER GOVERNMENT ACCORDING TO THEIR OWN WHIMS AND FANCIES.

IT IS A DIFFICULT JOB IN A TRYING TIME. MRS GANDHI CANNOT WAIT TO GET STARTED.

2

IN WHICH WE MEET THE ARTIST

Miss Reema Das was a little house-proud. On Saturday afternoon, while her roommate, the artist, snoozed in their shared bedroom, she tried to organize the attic. It was not easy. For one, the attic was tiny. For another, Piya's latest project—and her dramatic 'block' around it—had taken over the whole place. There were masses of books and photocopies everywhere, gathering dust; her easel stood in one corner; canvases with unfinished masterpieces (several of Mrs Gandhi at different stages of life) were stacked against every available wall; her desk had space only for her Mac, which meant all accessories, from paintbrushes to sketching pencils and a million post-its with comments, plus random objects meant to induce various moods, were all cluttering up the floor.

Still, Miss Das persevered with a broom and a cloth, sneezing intermittently as the dust rose in sudden bursts. Meanwhile, the cake rose gently in the oven, the samosas sat basking in the departing glow of the sun, and the day slipped into its finest phase. All was well. She hummed as she opened the door leading to the terrace and poured water on her plants. At five-thirty, exactly, the bell rang. Indira stood outside the door, with a tiffin box in hand and a scowl. Behind her, lurking in the shadow of the awning, was Happy Singh.

'Hello, Miss,' Happy said brightly.

'He insisted on coming,' Indira whispered wretchedly to Miss Das. 'I found him sitting outside the stationery shop, just like that. With nothing to do. And he decided to come. He doesn't believe in invitations or anything.'

Miss Das twinkled and said it was fine. She showed them inside.

Happy bounded in after Indira and quickly sat on the sofa, looking about him with a gentle curiosity. Indira, on the contrary, had her eyes popping out. The blood had rushed to her head.

So many books!

There were rows and rows *and* rows upon rows of books in bookshelves built on to the walls. She gingerly pushed back one or two books on the shelf closest to her and discovered there was another layer behind. She looked at Miss Das with a peculiar blend of horror and joy. 'Have you read *all* these books, Miss?'

'Oh no,' said a soft voice from behind.

It belonged to an ethereal person—a girl? a woman?—who seemed to have floated in from somewhere in blue pyjamas and a t-shirt with a half-eaten apple on it, and now chose to perch on the couch next to Happy. She had long hair piled in a messy bun on her head and a pencil was stuck in it. She shook her head seriously. 'It would be terrible if we'd already read all the books here. The very fact that there are so many unread books means there is so much happiness in the future that we have not yet tasted.' She smiled and, in an instant, Indira realized—with a swoosh of guilt—that her love for Miss Das was *nothing*, NOTHING, compared to what she felt for this floaty lady.

Miss Das rolled her eyes.

'Unfinished manuscripts mean the same, I suppose? Future happiness that we have not yet tasted? Indira, Happy, meet my roommate, Priyadarshini. Everyone calls her Piya.'

Indira smiled tentatively, trying desperately not to appear foolish. 'Namaste,' she said, as her mother had taught her. Happy gave a broad grin. 'Hello, Piya didi. You are an artist, no?'

'Miss Das has told us about you,' Indira now joined the conversation, intensely disliking the fact that Happy was butting in. He had promised to keep his mouth shut on the tortuous path from Basant Gaon to Vasant Vihar, while Indira was toying with the idea that she ought to wander about the neighbourhood randomly just to shake him off her trail. But that would have made her late.

'Ma has sent these,' Indira remembered, handing over the tiffin box to Piya didi, who opened it immediately. 'Aloo parathas! Ooh, let's eat.'

'Stop!' Miss Das grabbed the box out of her hands. 'First, we'll chat a bit. *Then* we'll eat the aloo parathas, with tea and cake, at 6:15. It's high tea.'

'Fine, Miss. As you wish, Miss,' said Piya, winking at the kids. 'What are we going to chat about, Miss?' She crossed her legs and looked at them.

Miss Das looked pointedly at Indira.

'Miss,' said Indira. 'Remember yesterday's assignment? I started writing it. You want to see?'

'But it's due only after the holidays,' said Happy, shocked. Though he shouldn't have been shocked. Indira's over-enthusiasm about homework was widely known. If only his mother had named him Indir Jeet or something, he could have happily copied Indira's assignment. Now, he would have to work on his own.

'What was the assignment?' Piya asked.

'*Write an essay around your name*,' Indira read from the top of the page, in her best reading-aloud voice. 'I have only a few lines.'

Miss Das nodded.

> My name is Indira Thapa.
>
> My name is taken from the name of the third prime minister of India, Indira Gandhi. Indira Gandhi was a great woman leader of our country. United States still has no woman president. But India had a woman prime minister in 1966. All countries in the world should learn from this. Because when a woman is the prime minister, everyone knows she cannot be fooled. Men can be fooled easily.

Indira interrupted her reading to shoot a meaningful glance at Happy.

'Now, now,' Miss Das murmured. 'Carry on, Indira.'

'Good point, though,' Piya didi said. 'About the US not having a woman president even now.'

Indira continued:

> Indira Gandhi was born in the city of Allahabad on 19 November 1917 and died on 31 October 1984 in New Delhi when two men, her own security guards, shot her. Her father was Jawaharlal

> Nehru, first prime minister of India. Her mother was Kamala Nehru, a freedom fighter. Her son was Rajiv Gandhi, also a prime minister. She was kind but also strict.
>
> I love Indira Gandhi.

Miss Das and Piya didi were both listening intently.

'...That's all I've got,' Indira said apologetically. 'The internet on the phone is very slow. Our cyber café has been closed since yesterday.'

'The café owner's wife's mother is very sick,' Happy supplied.

'There were many things on the Wikipedia page that I could not understand,' Indira said.

'That's not a problem, Indira. Piya can tell you everything about Mrs Gandhi, since you are interested. She's writing a book about her. She can explain all the things you didn't understand. But this is not what I had in mind, sweetheart. Remember what I said in class? Oral history?'

'I don't know what that means,' Indira mumbled.

'You didn't understand?' Happy said, looking at Indira. 'I did.'

'It means we record the views of people around us,' Miss Das said, 'Our family members, aged neighbours, people who have lived through what we now call "history". From their experiences we get a certain view of the past.'

'You are being too theoretical, Reema,' Piya interrupted. 'Indira, you should first ask your mother who named you. And then, go and ask that person why they named you Indira. That will give you a story about your family. But that story is, in some ways, more than just about your family. It says something about history, about the country. Everyone's memories together give us a picture of the country, like each bit in a jigsaw puzzle. My mother's mother, my Dida, named me Priyadarshini. She was a total Nehruvian and loved Mrs G. You know Priyadarshini was her second name?'

Indira nodded uncertainly.

Miss Das got up. 'You must do the same, Happy. Now let's have tea.'

'May I come with you to the kitchen?' Happy asked.

'Of course. Come help me.'

While Miss Das and Happy bantered with each other in the kitchen, Indira asked Piya didi, 'Are you writing a full book about Indira Gandhi?'

'I am supposed to,' Piya smiled sadly, 'but I am a little stuck.'

Together, they stepped out to the terrace. Miss Das had planned to serve tea on the white patio table under a brilliant pink umbrella. '2017 is Mrs Gandhi's centenary year. You know? She was born in 1917, as you said in your essay. A hundred years ago. I am in the process of creating a graphic book about her life.'

'What's a graphic book?'

'It tells a story the same way any book does. But with many more pictures than words. A bit like a comic.'

Indira digested this.

'So you know everything about her life?'

'Well,' said Piya, 'no one can know everything about anyone's life. Even their own. But yes, I have spent a whole year reading about Indira Gandhi's life, her times, letters she wrote to her father, to friends. I have studied her photographs. But... I have not finished the book yet.'

'Or even half of it,' Miss Das added darkly, as she walked towards them balancing a large tray in each hand. Happy followed, carrying the casserole of samosas in one hand and stuffing his mouth with the other.

The tea party grew merrier once the cake was unveiled and pronounced a big success. A little later, the guy with the red Nano arrived, and though both Indira and Happy would have liked to ignore him, he wormed his way into their hearts by cracking many jokes. His name was Rehaan. After the long dusk gave way to an inky night, he offered to drop the children home, since Miss Das and he were going to watch an all-night stand-up comedy show. 'Will Kapil Sharma be there?' Happy asked excitedly. 'I hope not,' said Rehaan, mock cuffing him.

Chattering about Kapil Sharma and 'improv', they trooped down. Indira lingered on the spiral staircase, where little twinkly lights had been hung during Diwali of last year and not been removed since. Piya didi pressed a little book into her hand. It was about the life of Indira Gandhi, mainly in photographs. 'Forget the internet. Read this instead. And here's our deal: when you tell me the oral history project of your name—' Indira giggled, 'I will show you some pages from my book. Okay?'

As the red Nano sped away from the drive, Piya savoured the buzzing in her body—the sense of blood pulsing in her temples. It was a good omen. This feeling always preceded good work. It had appeared after several weeks and she was afraid of scaring it away. She switched off her phone and the twinkly lights that sometimes lured in uninvited guests, made herself a cup of tea and sat down at her desk. It took her a while to select the right pencil. And then, with the ease of a practised swimmer, she jumped in, and instead of hitting her desk, she magically emerged in Allahabad, circa 1917.

She will take a tonga to Civil Lines, where mostly the British live. One Indian family has built a grand house there. It is called Anand Bhawan.

1917.

MARCH, MESOPOTAMIA.
WORLD WAR I: INDIAN TROOPS UNDER THE COMMAND OF LT. GEN. FRANCIS MAUD CAPTURE BAGHDAD ON BEHALF OF THE ALLIES.
APRIL, INDIA.
IN CHAMPARAN, MAHATMA GANDHI LAUNCHES THE CIVIL DISOBEDIENCE MOVEMENT AGAINST THE BRITISH FOR THE VERY FIRST TIME, PROTESTING THE TERRIBLE PLIGHT OF INDIGO FARMERS.
OCTOBER, RUSSIA.
THE BOLSHEVIK REVOLUTION, LED BY VLADIMIR ILYICH ULYANOV 'LENIN', DISRUPTS THE POLITICAL VOCABULARY OF THE WORLD FOREVER.

MEANWHILE, IN ALLAHABAD...
ON 19 NOVEMBER 1917, A DAUGHTER IS BORN TO THE IDEALISTIC YOUNG BARRISTER-TURNED-ASPIRING-FREEDOM-FIGHTER JAWAHARLAL NEHRU AND HIS CHARMING YOUNG WIFE, KAMALA. THEY CALL HER INDIRA PRIYADARSHINI.

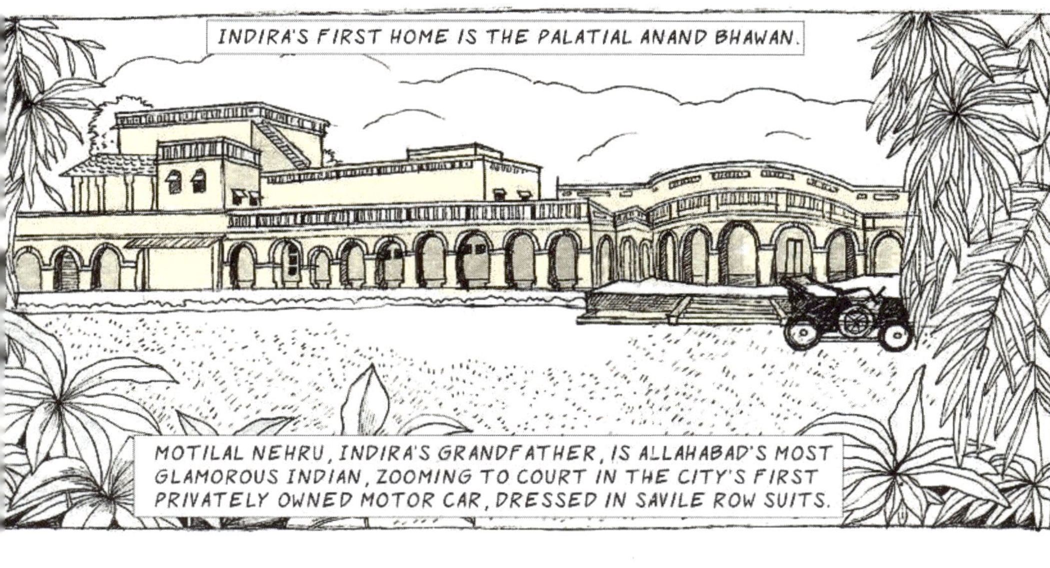
INDIRA'S FIRST HOME IS THE PALATIAL ANAND BHAWAN.
MOTILAL NEHRU, INDIRA'S GRANDFATHER, IS ALLAHABAD'S MOST GLAMOROUS INDIAN, ZOOMING TO COURT IN THE CITY'S FIRST PRIVATELY OWNED MOTOR CAR, DRESSED IN SAVILE ROW SUITS.

MOTILAL LOVES TO ENTERTAIN EXTRAVAGANTLY. THE DINING ROOM AT ANAND BHAWAN SEES GUESTS, INDIAN AND BRITISH, ALMOST EVERY SINGLE EVENING. TWO KINDS OF CUISINES ARE SERVED, INDIAN AND CONTINENTAL.
EH, RAM PRASAD, THAT'S THE WRONG WINE GLASS YOU'RE USING. WANT TO GET FIRED OR WHAT?
INDIRA PRIYADARSHINI'S BIRTH BRINGS GREAT JOY TO THE FAMILY.
IF THE GRANDMOTHER AND HER CIRCLE OF WOMEN MURMUR...
IT SHOULD HAVE BEEN A BOY...
MOTILAL SILENCES THEM WITH A CUSTOMARY ROAR.

BB... BUT...
THERE IS ALSO AN INDIAN VEGETARIAN KITCHEN RUN BY MOTILAL'S WIFE, SWARUP RANI, IN HER PART OF THE HOUSE. HERE, TRADITIONAL KASHMIRI PANDIT MEALS ARE COOKED AND EATEN.
THIS GIRL WILL BE EQUAL TO A THOUSAND SONS!

IN THE EARLY YEARS OF INDIRA'S LIFE, ANAND BHAWAN SEETHES WITH RESENTMENT. THE MINOR WARS ARE IN THE WOMEN'S WORLDS. JAWAHARLAL'S ADORED SISTERS, SARUP (LATER VIJAYLAKSHMI) AND KRISHNA, HAVE BEEN BROUGHT UP BY BRITISH GOVERNESSES AND ARE VERY ANGLICIZED. THE YOUNG BAHU, KAMALA, COMES FROM A DEEPLY CONSERVATIVE KASHMIRI FAMILY IN OLD DELHI. DESPITE EFFORTS TO INTEGRATE, KAMALA REMAINS A PERENNIAL OUTSIDER.
UFF, KAMALA IS PULLING A LONG FACE AGAIN. SOON SHE WILL SAY SHE IS FEELING ILL.
BUT THE TENSIONS OF THE ZENANA ARE NOTHING COMPARED TO WHAT IS HAPPENING BETWEEN FATHER AND SON.

IN DECEMBER 1916, JAWAHARLAL, RESTLESS AND CONFLICTED IN HIS POLITICS, HAD COME UNDER THE SWAY OF MAHATMA GANDHI. HE WAS TO WRITE LATER ABOUT THAT MOMENT: 'AND THEN GANDHI CAME... HE DID NOT DESCEND FROM THE TOP, HE SEEMED TO EMERGE FROM THE MILLIONS OF INDIA.'
AS GANDHI'S INFLUENCE BEGINS TO COMPLETELY RESHAPE HIS ADORED ONLY SON'S VIEWS, MOTILAL BECOMES INCREASINGLY BELLIGERENT.
I'VE HAD ENOUGH OF YOUR AND YOUR M.K. GANDHI'S MIDSUMMER MADNESS. CIVIL DISOBEDIENCE WILL DISLODGE THE MIGHTY BRITISH!?! YOU HAVE A WIFE AND CHILD NOW, JAWAHARLAL. ENOUGH IDEALISM! DON YOUR ROBES, EARN MONEY, SPEND IT.
BUT THEN, IN 1919...

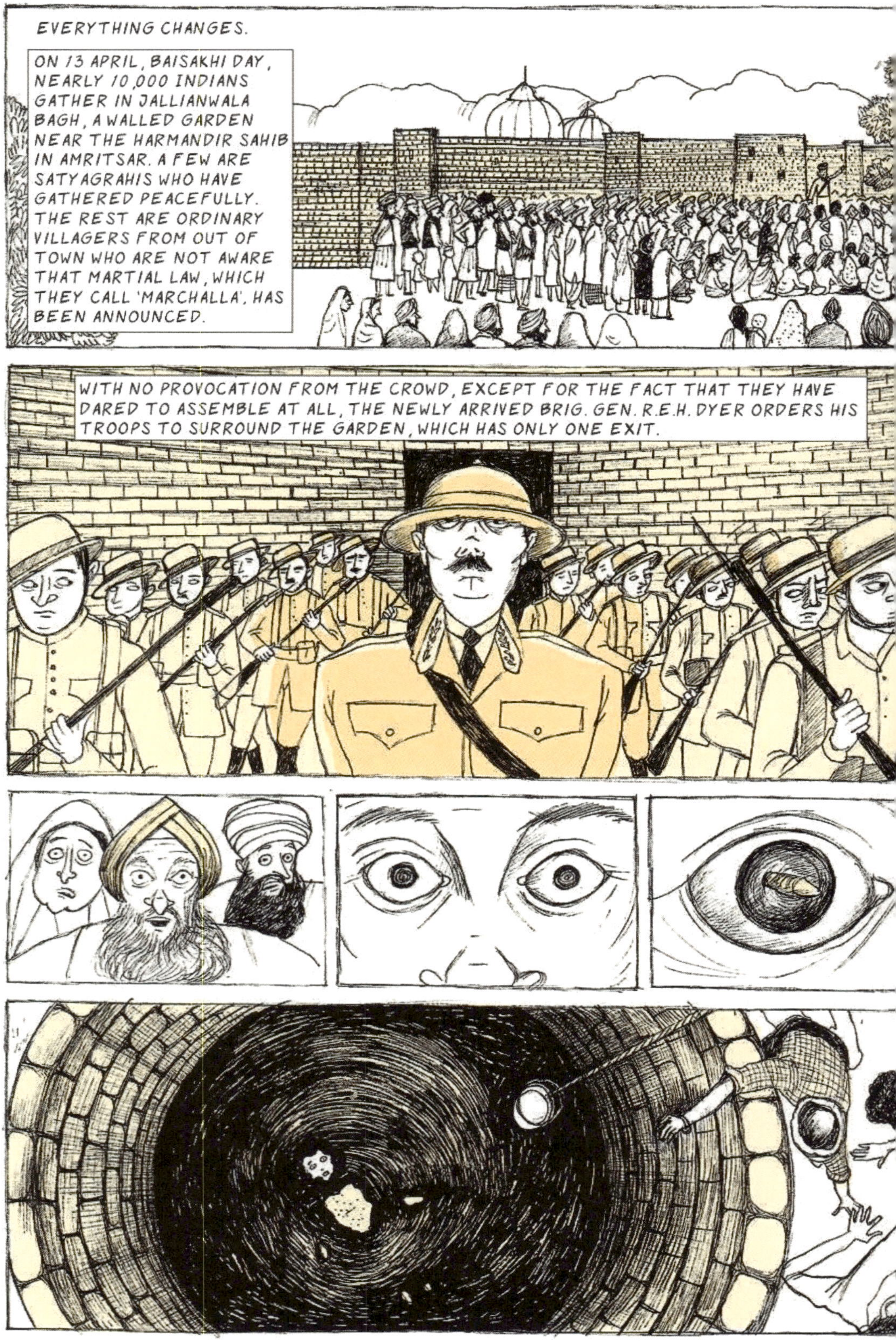
EVERYTHING CHANGES.
ON 13 APRIL, BAISAKHI DAY, NEARLY 10,000 INDIANS GATHER IN JALLIANWALA BAGH, A WALLED GARDEN NEAR THE HARMANDIR SAHIB IN AMRITSAR. A FEW ARE SATYAGRAHIS WHO HAVE GATHERED PEACEFULLY. THE REST ARE ORDINARY VILLAGERS FROM OUT OF TOWN WHO ARE NOT AWARE THAT MARTIAL LAW, WHICH THEY CALL 'MARCHALLA', HAS BEEN ANNOUNCED.
WITH NO PROVOCATION FROM THE CROWD, EXCEPT FOR THE FACT THAT THEY HAVE DARED TO ASSEMBLE AT ALL, THE NEWLY ARRIVED BRIG. GEN. R.E.H. DYER ORDERS HIS TROOPS TO SURROUND THE GARDEN, WHICH HAS ONLY ONE EXIT.

1600 ROUNDS HAVE BEEN EXHAUSTED. 379 PEOPLE ARE DEAD, AND 1137 WOUNDED.

WHAT DYER DOES NOT ANTICIPATE IS THAT THE SHOTS WILL ECHO ACROSS THE SUBCONTINENT. IN REMOTE AREAS OF INDIA, PEOPLE HEAR OF THE KILLINGS, OF THE TERROR UNLEASHED BY THE ANGREZ. IN MANY HOMES, PEOPLE REFUSE TO EAT THAT NIGHT.

IN ANAND BHAWAN, A POINT OF NO RETURN IS REACHED AND MOTILAL NEHRU EMBRACES SATYAGRAHA WHOLE-HEARTEDLY.
IN SEPTEMBER 1920, THREE-YEAR-OLD INDIRA ACCOMPANIES HER GRANDFATHER AND FATHER TO A SPECIAL SESSION OF THE CONGRESS, WHERE MAHATMA GANDHI GIVES THE CLARION CALL FOR SWARAJ VIA SWADESHI.

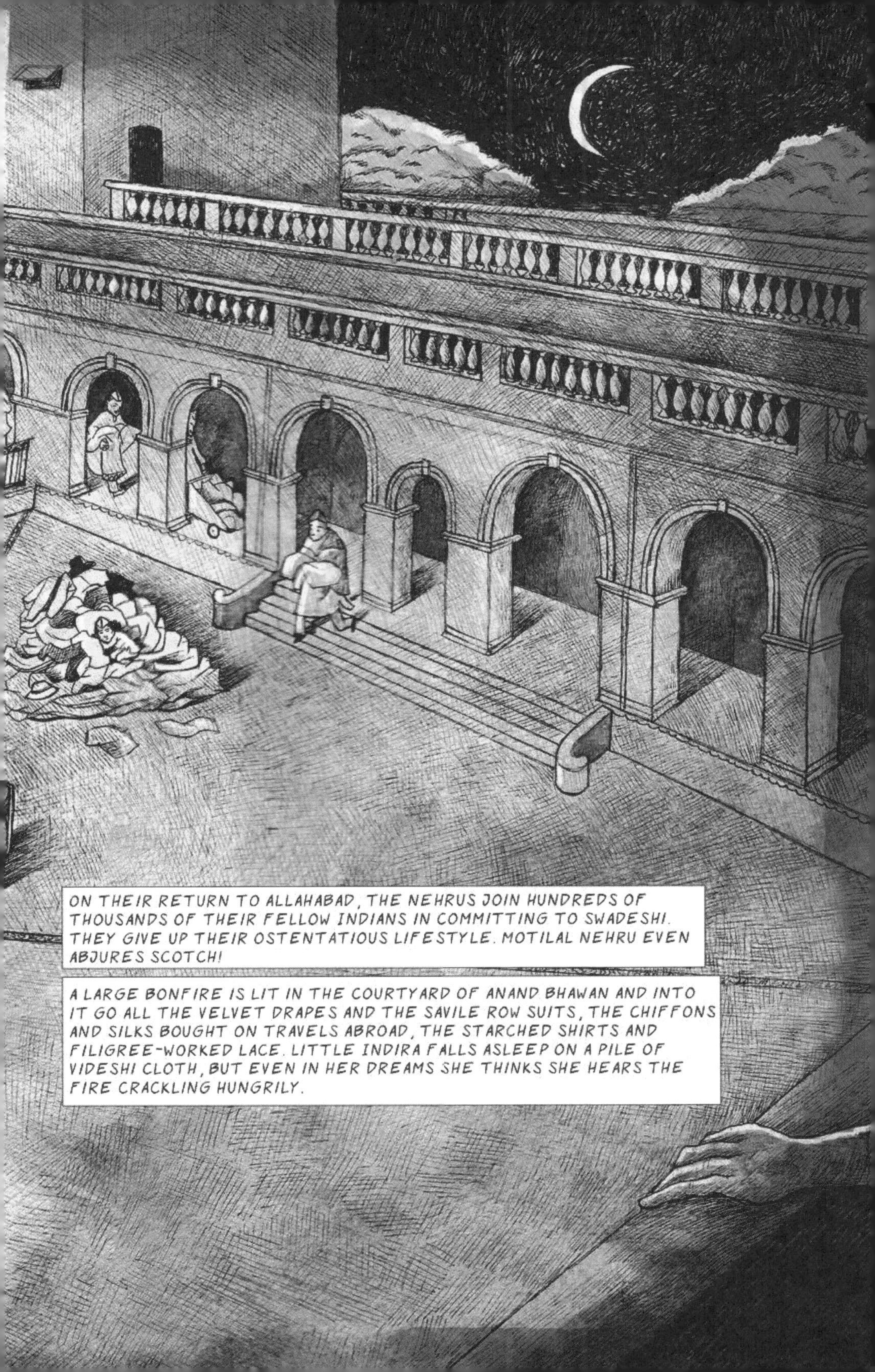
ON THEIR RETURN TO ALLAHABAD, THE NEHRUS JOIN HUNDREDS OF THOUSANDS OF THEIR FELLOW INDIANS IN COMMITTING TO SWADESHI. THEY GIVE UP THEIR OSTENTATIOUS LIFESTYLE. MOTILAL NEHRU EVEN ABJURES SCOTCH!
A LARGE BONFIRE IS LIT IN THE COURTYARD OF ANAND BHAWAN AND INTO IT GO ALL THE VELVET DRAPES AND THE SAVILE ROW SUITS, THE CHIFFONS AND SILKS BOUGHT ON TRAVELS ABROAD, THE STARCHED SHIRTS AND FILIGREE-WORKED LACE. LITTLE INDIRA FALLS ASLEEP ON A PILE OF VIDESHI CLOTH, BUT EVEN IN HER DREAMS SHE THINKS SHE HEARS THE FIRE CRACKLING HUNGRILY.

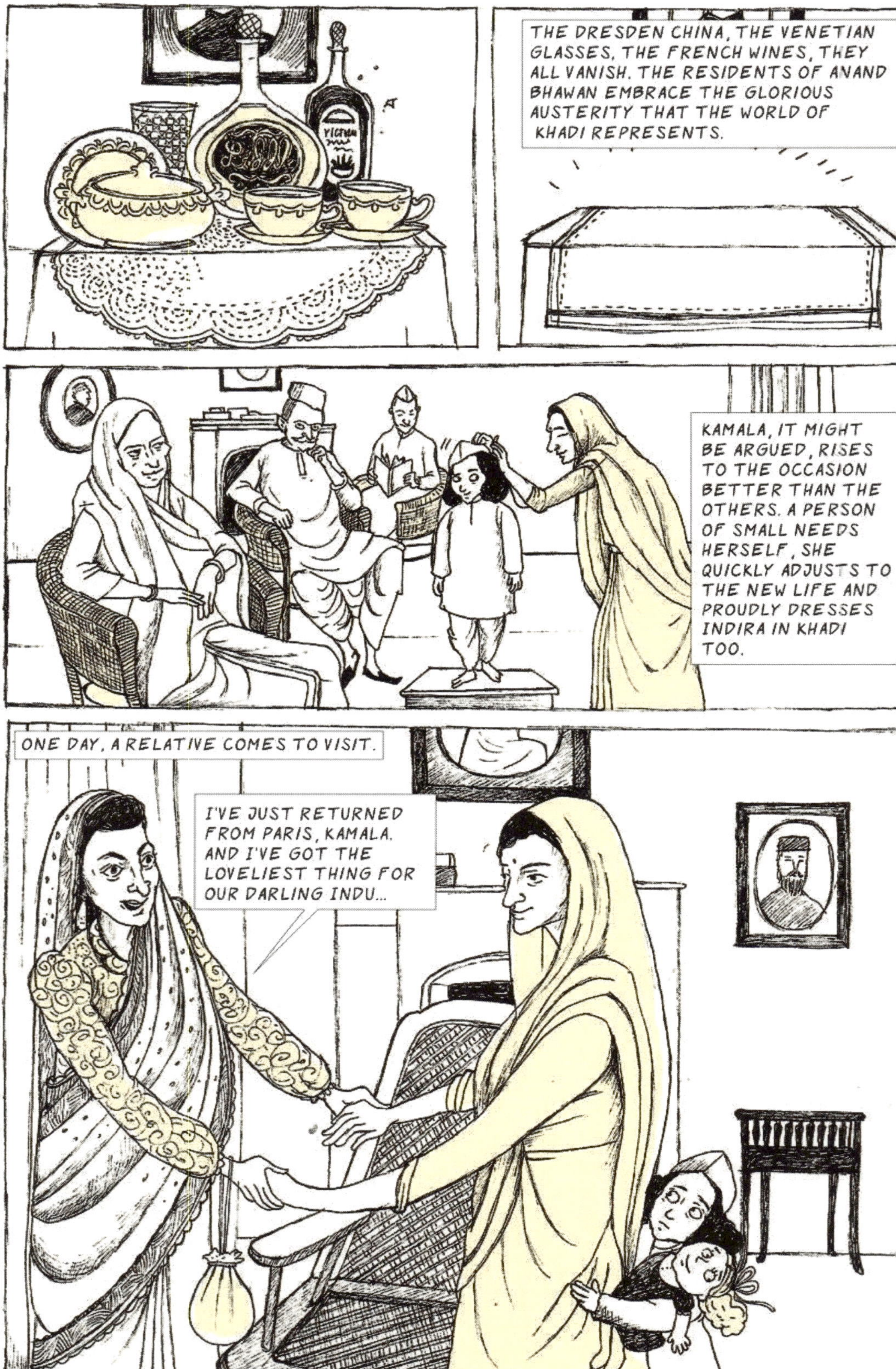
THE DRESDEN CHINA, THE VENETIAN GLASSES, THE FRENCH WINES, THEY ALL VANISH. THE RESIDENTS OF ANAND BHAWAN EMBRACE THE GLORIOUS AUSTERITY THAT THE WORLD OF KHADI REPRESENTS.
KAMALA, IT MIGHT BE ARGUED, RISES TO THE OCCASION BETTER THAN THE OTHERS. A PERSON OF SMALL NEEDS HERSELF, SHE QUICKLY ADJUSTS TO THE NEW LIFE AND PROUDLY DRESSES INDIRA IN KHADI TOO.
ONE DAY, A RELATIVE COMES TO VISIT.
I'VE JUST RETURNED FROM PARIS, KAMALA, AND I'VE GOT THE LOVELIEST THING FOR OUR DARLING INDU...

THE PARIS-RETURNEE HAS BROUGHT INDU A BEAUTIFUL EMBROIDERED FROCK.
THE PURRFECT COLOUR FOR INDU'S COMPLEXION TOO.
BHABHIJI, WE ONLY WEAR HANDSPUN CLOTH NOW. PLEASE FORGIVE OUR INABILITY TO ACCEPT THIS PRESENT. IT'S YOUR THOUGHT THAT COUNTS...
KAMALA, YOUR SKIN HAS BECOME RED BECAUSE OF THIS ROUGH CLOTH, TSK TSK. DO WHAT YOU WANT BY ALL MEANS (THOUGH IT'S MADNESS!) BUT WHY MAKE THE CHILD SUFFER?
COME HERE, INDU.
CHACHI HAS BROUGHT THIS FOREIGN-MADE FROCK FOR YOU. IT IS VERY PRETTY AND YOU CAN WEAR IT IF YOU LIKE. BUT TELL ME, DO YOU REMEMBER THAT BIG FIRE IN WHICH WE BURNT ALL OUR FOREIGN CLOTH?
WOULD YOU LIKE TO WEAR THIS WHEN THE REST OF US ARE WEARING KHADI?
TAKE IT AWAY! I SHAN'T WEAR IT!
GOOD FOR YOU, MISS SAINT. BUT WHAT ABOUT THAT FOREIGN DOLL IN YOUR ARMS?
THE NEXT FEW DAYS FEEL LIKE WEEKS, LIKE MONTHS, LIKE YEARS.

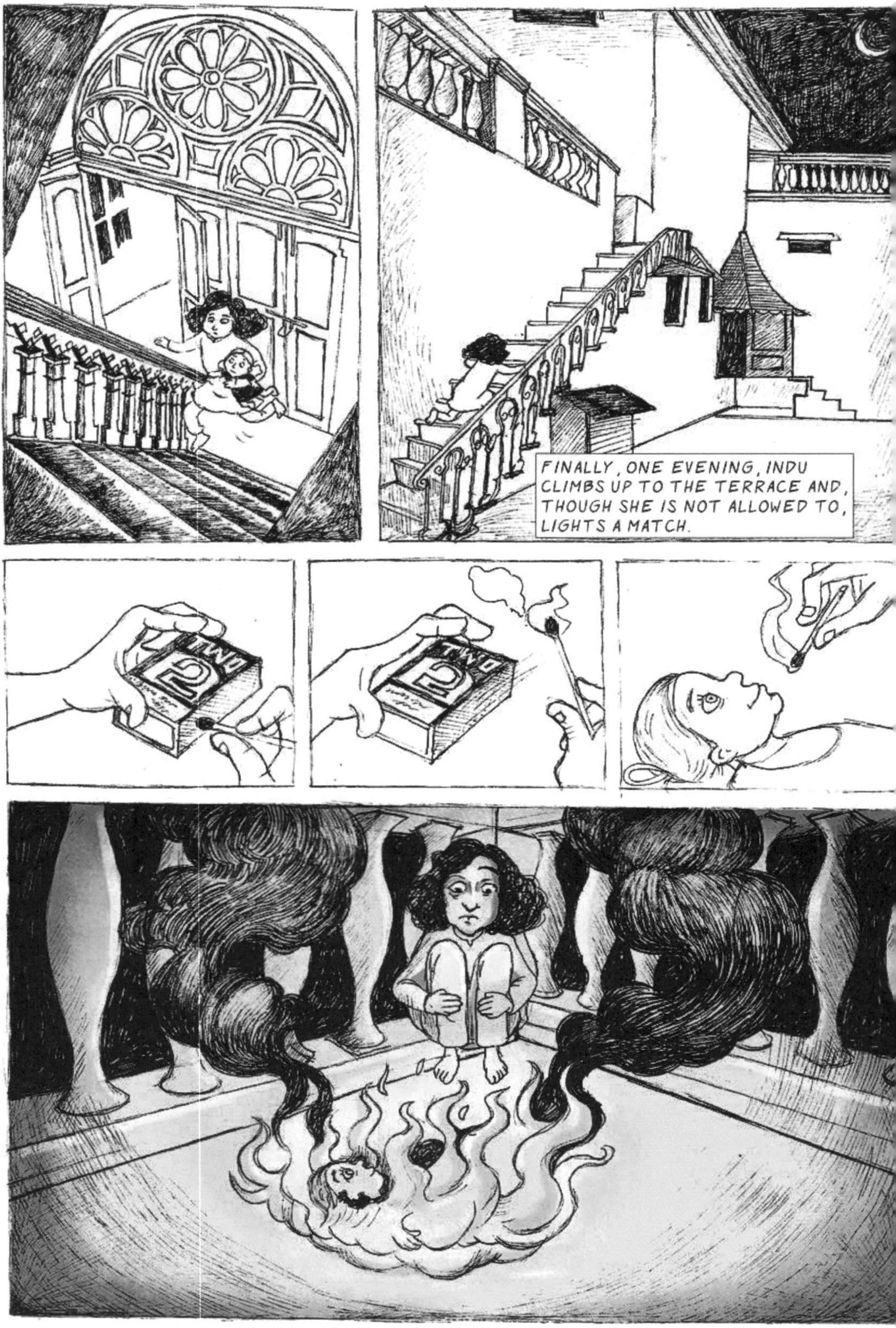
FINALLY, ONE EVENING, INDU CLIMBS UP TO THE TERRACE AND, THOUGH SHE IS NOT ALLOWED TO, LIGHTS A MATCH.

SOMETHING CHANGES INSIDE HER FOREVER.
NOTHING VALUABLE CAN BE ATTAINED WITHOUT SACRIFICE.
THAT NIGHT, SHE COMES DOWN WITH A HIGH FEVER.

3

IN WHICH WE MEET A VERY IMPORTANT PERSON

'So sorry to disturb you,' Indira repeated, fanning herself vigorously with an old map of Delhi.

Indira Thapa, of Class VI (A), Sarvodaya Kanya Vidyalaya No. 18, was sitting under the awning of a church, just beneath the large stained-glass window that did not open. In front of her, down Poorvi Marg, a stream of cars and buses glided past, sunlight bouncing off their sleek bodies. All she had to do, she told herself, was walk down the lane next to the church, turn left at the last house, open the second gate, climb up the spiral staircase and knock. Then say, 'Sorry to disturb you, Miss. Sorry to disturb you, Piya didi.'

Truth is, the summer vacation was killing her.

School was out and so were tuitions. Ma was away for most of the day. She had read the three novels she had managed to salvage from the fire at least a hundred times: two Enid Blytons and one Roald Dahl. As for the Indira Gandhi picture book Piya didi had given her—she had read it several times in the last few days, and could now close her eyes and remember details: the picture of the old house, Indira Gandhi petting a red panda, Indira Gandhi giving a speech to thousands of people. She had also re-read the entire stack of *Chandamama* magazines that her mother's boss, Mrs Tandon, had given her last year, re-laughed at the Hindi jokes, re-solved the puzzles inside and even coloured the pictures in desperation, though everyone knew colouring was for kids. She had tried reading the dictionary too—but that was plain depressing.

Their little room got so severely hot in the afternoon that she went upstairs and sat on the landing outside the terrace. Though the roof was burning, a little breeze crept into the stairway. Ma was planning to buy a cooler as soon as she got her salary this month. But for now, it felt so stuffy that Indira got more and more agitated every hour. Today, when Ma had to go back after lunch, Indira announced she was going for a walk.

'A walk?' Arati was shocked. Indian children didn't go out for walks! Also, didn't she know this was Delhi? The most unsafe city in India?

'A walk to Piya didi and Miss Das's!' Indira said, though she hadn't really planned that far ahead. 'I didn't finish!'

'Oh, that's fine,' Ma said. 'That distance you can walk. Why don't you take Happy along too?'

Indira rolled her eyes. Like hell she would take Happy along.

'But don't disturb them too much. Okay?'

Indira hurried down the warren of lanes to C Block, humming to herself, past the market, past the beautiful mansions and large well-paved streets, past the green parks that were so pretty and cool, even in the heat. Though rivulets of sweat were running down her back, there was a light breeze outside that fanned her hair and made her feel a little like Alia Bhatt. But after she reached the church, she began to feel hesitant. Piya didi and Miss Das hadn't invited her *exactly*. Would it be rude if she just dropped by? The oral history project was not yet done because her Dadaji was away at her uncle's house in Nepal. Maybe Piya didi would show her some pages of her Indira Gandhi book anyway? Plus, she had to return the book Piya didi had lent her.

That settled, Indira bounced up from the concrete plinth, said goodbye to the nice guava seller who sat outside the church, smoothed down her blue frock, swished her hair back and marched towards her destination. 'Sorry to disturb you,' she muttered, and a couple of cows eating garbage looked up with their liquid brown eyes and flicked their tails at the vision in blue.

As it happened, Indira didn't need to knock. The door was open and a grown-up sounding voice wafted out.

'Piya, you do realize that we can't all be vague about these things? I need firm dates so I can ask the copyeditors to clear their schedule, I need to make a plan for production, block the press…' M was saying sternly, eyes flashing. Indira stood tentatively outside. 'There are other biographies being published too. Of course, given that people don't read books anymore, only "lists", I think our book has a better shot at numbers than the weighty biographies. But only if you finish it, Piya. I am getting quite worried.'

'I do, I really truly do want to finish it soon,' Piya replied, twisting the end of her plait around her fingers in a tortured way. 'There's someone at the door, I think. Just a second please.'

One doesn't know if Piya was expecting a magical intervention from some mysterious source to save her from the sobering discussion inside, but it would appear from the manner in which her face lit up that Indira was, in fact, exactly what the cosmos had ordered. 'Come in, come in,' she said. 'I was thinking of you all week.'

Then she lowered her voice and whispered, 'I'm afraid I'm in big trouble.'

'I can hear you,' M's voice rang out.

M had got up from her chair in the meantime and picked up a stack of sketches from Piya's desk in the corner. She rummaged in her bag for her spectacles and started looking at the images closely, the whole transition from Indu to Mrs Gandhi, through different moods, odd angles, gentle lights.

Indira and Piya both sat nervously on the couch.

Finally, M looked up. 'And who do we have here?' she asked, allowing herself a brief smile.

'This is Indira,' Piya replied. 'Remember I told you about the young girl who helped me finish Chapter Two? My impromptu muse? Indira, this is M. My publisher. A very important person.'

'Hello, Indira,' M said.

M had short wavy hair, a straight nose, grey eyes. She wore a silk dupatta whose colours were weird—a pink that seemed to shimmer into a blue, with gentle stripes that could be grey *or* purple. 'Hello,' Indira mumbled.

'There's no need for you to be scared of me. You are Reema's student?'

'Yes,' Indira mumbled.

'Good,' said M. 'Thank god for Reema. You know your Piya didi was dodging my calls all month. Fortunately I met Reema at that comedy event and got her to set this up. Now. Indira, how would you like to help your Piya didi finish the book?'

'I would love to.'

'Good. Come here. Look at these pages.'

Indira pulled up a chair next to M.

'Maybe I should make some tea,' Piya said, chewing her lip. She went to the terrace and plucked some tulsi leaves, silently apologising to the plant.

Indira touched the pages hesitantly. They were large and so beautifully drawn that you almost couldn't believe they were made by hand. On the first page, there were panels with images she didn't quite understand: a band in London, a tall, black man in Chicago, all these other people in India. But then, on the next page, there she was—Indira Gandhi!

'These are the drawings. Now let me show you the versions where the story has been added. You'll understand it better.'

M took out a silver laptop from her bag—Indira had never seen anything so thin and light and beautiful—and quickly whipped out some images.

Piya had wandered back in.

'Should I turn the AC on?' she asked M. 'Sorry, I forgot.'

'That's okay,' M said. 'It's not like a single AC can cool a Delhi barsaati in summer. You know the writer Ruchir Joshi? He wrote a humorous article about it.'

'What did you do to the drawings, Piya didi?' Indira asked.

'Oh, I scanned them. Then I added the text to each panel. The text is a different layer, so I can remove it quite easily too. And then I added colour. That I did using computer tools, only later.'

'Oh,' said Indira, not quite understanding much of the process, though she'd never admit that. She hunched over the computer reading the pages. Once she saw the accompanying text, everything began to make sense. Well, not everything. She didn't know the Beatles—or this Martin Luther person. But because of the images, she had a sense of everything. It was January 1966. She counted on her fingers to be sure—fifty years ago.

'Piya didi, how do you know exactly what Mrs Gandhi did that morning fifty years ago?'

'Oh, well, you know... some of it is recorded. She went to Raj Ghat, she went to Shanti Vana, Teen Murti; Subhadra Joshi pinned that rose on her sari; these things are known. The rest of it is... my imagination. A slight amount of condensing happens, so I say Raj Ghat and Teen Murti, but leave out Shanti Vana. Even while "inventing" the truth, though, you anchor every single thing in real details. Her house on 1 Safdarjung Road has these same arched windows. Her staff from Allahabad called her "Bibiji". And she *did* tell Bapu that this whole business of brahmacharya after marriage was absurd!'

'Piya didi?' Indira spoke again, a few minutes later. 'What is the Syndicate?'

Piya replied, 'Well, it seems the "Syndicate" was a small group of senior Congress ministers. There was K. Kamaraj, the Congress President, Atulya Ghosh from West Bengal, S.K. Patil, Sanjiva Reddy, S. Nijalingappa . . . a few of them are in that image of the PM aspirants. Towards the beginning of the chapter?'

'Wait, I want to read from the beginning again. Please?'

M showed her how the Mac could be operated.

As Indira read on, the expressions on her face changed. M gazed at her open face, her lips slightly parted in concentration, and her own face softened. She got up and walked outside. The sun was now closer to the horizon and a bunch of parakeets were chattering in the tree that shook red flowers onto the terrace every evening.

When Piya brought her a cup of tea, M said, 'Sweetheart, you *do* realize that we need the book to come out when there's maximum noise around it? The centenary celebration will ensure...'

Piya brushed away the words with a flamboyant shrug.

'M,' she said. 'I just solved a problem. You know how I was stuck with Chapter Three for the longest time? Just how could I tell the story of Mrs G's early years without making it chronological and dull? Young people these days don't like chronological narratives anyway. You know how you were complaining that nobody reads books anymore, that millennials only read lists?'

'Yes.' M nodded uncertainly, not sure where this was going.

'Eight Things to Do in Paris in Winter. Twenty-three Things That Only People Who Wear Glasses Will Understand. Twelve Ways to Annoy Your Publisher.'

'Exactly,' said Piya triumphantly. 'I'll do a list!'

'I don't understand,' said M. 'I'm too old, I think. List, no list, just remember I'll need the full and final manuscript soon. Only then can I put it on the schedule. Piya, are you listening to me?'

'We'll call it: Seven Things That Will Happen to You if Your Parents are Freedom Fighters. I'll need to go to Allahabad to do it properly.'

'Hmm, okay. Go to Allahabad. Take your young muse with you. And Reema—please take Reema. She'll ensure you get the bloody pages done.'

SEVEN THINGS THAT WILL HAPPEN TO YOU IF YOU BELONG TO A FAMILY OF FREEDOM FIGHTERS.

#ONE

YOU WILL GET USED TO PRISON SENTENCES BEING HANDED DOWN AT THE DROP OF A HAT.

#TWO
YOU WILL LEARN TO DEFEND YOUR PARENTS AND THEIR IDEALISM TO ALL KINDS OF PEOPLE.
SWARUP RANI'S WIDOWED SISTER BIBI AMMA RULES OVER ANAND BHAWAN WITH AN IRON FIST AND AN ACID TONGUE.
IT'S ALL KAMALA'S FAULT! HAD SHE NOT BEEN SWEPT AWAY BY ALL THIS NATIONALISM NONSENSE, JAWAHAR WOULD HAVE BEEN A REGULAR HOUSEHOLDER TOO.
THAT'S RIDICULOUS! MUMMIE KNOWS PAPU IS DOING THIS FOR A GREATER CAUSE...
GRADUALLY, THERE COMES ABOUT A REVERSAL OF ROLES. AS KAMALA BEGINS TO FALL ILL MORE AND MORE FREQUENTLY (THE JEALOUSY AND SNIPING AT HOME DO NOT HELP) AND JAWAHARLAL HAS LONGER STINTS IN PRISON, INDU BECOMES A QUASI-PARENT TO HER BULLIED-AND-HURT MOTHER AND WORKAHOLIC-IDEALIST-BAD-HOUSEHOLDER FATHER. THIS PATTERN PERSISTS TO THE END OF THEIR LIVES.

#THREE
YOU WILL BE REQUIRED TO PROVE YOURSELF IN NOVEL WAYS.
DECEMBER 1928. THE ANNUAL CONGRESS SESSION IN CALCUTTA IS TO BE CHAIRED BY MOTILAL NEHRU. THE ENTIRE FAMILY ACCOMPANIES HIM THERE. AT HOWRAH STATION, MOTILAL IS RECEIVED WITH A 101-GUN SALUTE, AND THEN TAKEN THROUGH THE CITY IN A CARRIAGE DRAWN BY TWENTY-EIGHT WHITE HORSES. LEADING THE PROCESSION IS A DYNAMIC YOUNG SUBHAS CHANDRA BOSE, THE 'GENERAL OFFICER COMMANDING' OF THE VOLUNTEER CORPS.
WATCHING THE PAGEANTRY IS AN EIGHT YEAR OLD WHO WILL LATER BECOME A POLITICIAN HIMSELF: SIDDHARTHA SHANKAR RAY, A GRANDSON OF THE LATE C.R. DAS. HE IS THE LEADER OF A PACK OF CONGRESS KIDS WHO ARE WAITING EAGERLY FOR A GLIMPSE OF...

INDIRA NEHRU? IS THAT REALLY HER? SHE LOOKS SO THIN AND... UNIMPORTANT!
THE NEXT MORNING, TO REDEEM HER IMAGE, INDIRA FORCES HERSELF TO EAT HALF-A-DOZEN BANANAS AT BREAKFAST.
WHILE PURNA SWARAJ VS DOMINION STATUS IS BITTERLY ARGUED AT THE CALCUTTA CONGRESS...
... IN CERTAIN CIRCLES THE CONVERSATION REVOLVES AROUND...
6 BANANAS? REALLY?
MAYBE 7 OR 8... I DIDN'T COUNT.
MANY MANY YEARS LATER, WHEN MRS GANDHI IS THE PRIME MINISTER OF INDIA AND ATTENDS THE CONGRESS SESSION IN CALCUTTA IN 1972, CHIEF MINISTER SIDDHARTHA SHANKAR RAY PLANTS A BANANA TREE OUTSIDE HER WINDOW.
INDU, HOW MANY WHITE HORSES WERE THERE THAT DAY? 28? 31?
FELT LIKE 200!

#FOUR
YOU WILL START AN ORGANIZATION OF YOUR OWN BEFORE YOU ARE THIRTEEN.
IT IS THE SPRING OF 1930. THE EFFECTS OF MAHATMA GANDHI'S DANDI MARCH ARE FELT ACROSS THE NATION.
WHY CAN'T I JOIN THE CONGRESS? I TOOK THE OATH OF PURNA SWARAJ AT THE LAHORE SESSION, DIDN'T I?
YOU HAVE TO BE 18, INDU. NO, SORRY, AT LEAST 21.
GANDHI'S MARCH BEGINS FOR LIBERTY
WAIT, I SHALL MAKE MY OWN CONGRESS. AND I SHAN'T LET ANYONE ABOVE 18, NO, 21, ENROLL!
PATRIOTIC (OR AT LEAST ENTHUSIASTIC) CHILDREN FROM ALL OVER ALLAHABAD ARE DRAFTED INTO THE 'VANAR SENA' BY INDU.
WHEN THE CONGRESS ANNOUNCES A DEMONSTRATION WEEK ACROSS THE COUNTRY, IN ALLAHABAD, INDIRA LEADS A MARCH OF 15,000 CHILDREN THAT ENDS IN ANAND BHAWAN WITH HER FIRST PUBLIC ADDRESS.

SHE CHANNELS HER INNER JOAN OF ARC AND MAKES AN IMPASSIONED PLEA FOR INDEPENDENCE.
SINCE HER VOICE DOES NOT GO AS FAR AS HER VOCABULARY DOES, B.N. PANDE, THE 'HONORARY LANGOOR' AMONG THE VANARS, ACTS AS HER HUMAN MICROPHONE.
BHARAT MATA KI JAI!
BHARAT MATA KI JAI!

INDU BRINGS HER PARENTS' SERIOUSNESS TO THE AFFAIRS OF THE VANAR SENA.

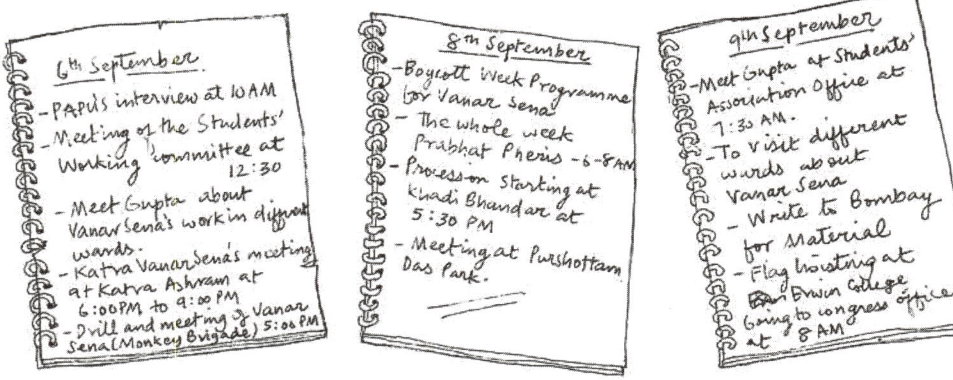

PAPU HEARS OF THE MONKEY BRIGADE IN PRISON...
INDU DEAR, CONGRATULATIONS TO THE LITTLE MONKEY IN ENROLLING FELLOW VANARS IN THE VANAR SENA!
MOTILAL NEHRU IS EVEN MORE TAKEN WITH INDU'S NEW PROJECT.
I SUGGEST EACH WARRIOR SHOULD WEAR A TAIL PROPORTIONATE TO THEIR RANK. WHAT SAY, INDU?
QUICKLY, SHE REALIZES THAT THE GREATEST UTILITY OF THE VANAR SENA IS AS A GRASSROOTS INTELLIGENCE AGENCY.
OLICE STATION
PSST... LISTEN!
LAL BAHADUR SHASTRI DESERVES A VISIT FROM US. NO?
HMM. TINY MAN, TOO MUCH ENERGY!
CHACHA, THERE'S A LETTER FOR YOU, ABOUT SHASTRIJI.
LATER, AS PRIME MINISTER, INDU WILL GO ON TO FOUND INDIA'S EXTERNAL INTELLIGENCE AGENCY, THE RESEARCH AND ANALYSIS WING (R&AW), IN 1968.

#FIVE
YOU WILL MEET THE LOVE OF YOUR LIFE AT A DEMONSTRATION.
INDU HAS NO IDEA THAT A HOT SUMMER'S DAY IN 1930 WILL CHANGE HER LIFE FOREVER.
BHARAT MATA KI JAI!
ARRE YAAR! HERE THEY GO AGAIN. CAN'T EVEN BUNK CLASS IN PEACE.
MAHATMA GANDHI KI JAI!
HAHA! FEROZE, WE SHOULD ASK THEM TO FIGHT FOR OUR FREEDOM FROM PROFESSOR MISTRY.
EWING CHRISTIAN COLLEGE, WHERE KAMALA NEHRU, ACCOMPANIED BY KRISHNA AND INDU, WERE PICKETING, IS ALSO YOUNG FEROZE GANDHI'S ADDA.
ALL OF A SUDDEN, OVERCOME BY THE HEAT OF THE AIRLESS DAY, KAMALA FAINTS.
OH MY GOD, KAMALA... HELP!
HEY! HEY! LOOKS LIKE THERE'S TROUBLE.

THERE IS TROUBLE AND HOW! AFTER KAMALA REVIVES, FEROZE ACCOMPANIES THE LADIES HOME. IN THE CHAOS, IT IS NOT KNOWN IF INDIRA OR FEROZE REGISTER EACH OTHER'S PRESENCE, BUT THIS IS THEIR FIRST MEETING.
THE NEXT DAY, FEROZE GANDHI COMES TO ANAND BHAWAN, APOLOGISES FOR HIS CAVALIER BEHAVIOUR, AND ASKS TO BE INITIATED INTO THE MYSTICAL TRADITIONS OF SATYAGRAHA. SOON HE IS A CARD-CARRYING, KHADI-WEARING CONGRESS WORKER.
A FEW MONTHS LATER, THE VANAR SENA ORGANIZES A FLAG HOISTING.
SHE'S THIN AS A WISP, BUT THE GIRL'S GOT SPUNK!
AFTERWARDS, FEROZE GIVES HER STICKY SWEETS AS A PRIZE. IT WILL BE MANY YEARS, THOUGH, BEFORE INDIRA AGREES TO GIVE HIM HER HEART.
Parry's
Parry's

#SIX
YOU WILL GO TO MORE EDUCATIONAL INSTITUTES THAN YOU CAN COUNT. IN THE FINAL ANALYSIS, YOU WILL HAVE LEARNT FROM THE UNIVERSITY OF LIFE.
1922 Modern School, Delhi
1924, St Cecilia's, Allahabad
इन्दुजी।
पापू का प्यार
L' Ecole Internationale, 1926
Jail.
PRISONER'S LETTER.
Alipore Central Jail
Calcutta

IN LETTER AFTER LETTER, JAWAHARLAL AND KAMALA FRET ABOUT INDU'S EDUCATION. IN LETTER AFTER LETTER, PAPU AND INDU DISCUSS BOOKS THEY ARE READING, AND KAMALA AND INDU TALK OF DISCIPLINE AND LIFE, AND IT BECOMES APPARENT SOON THAT IN MOST MATTERS INDIRA IS AN AUTO DIDACT.

SHE GOES TO SCHOOLS IN ALLAHABAD, GENEVA, THE SWISS COUNTRYSIDE, MONTANA, POONA, BOMBAY AND BRISTOL. SHE ATTENDS COLLEGE IN SHANTINIKETAN, WHERE SHE LEARNS DANCING, AND OXFORD, WHERE THE INDIA LEAGUE CONSUMES HER TIME. HOWEVER, IN NEITHER PLACE IS SHE ABLE TO STAY LONG ENOUGH TO EARN A DEGREE. SHE LEAVES SHANTINIKETAN TO ACCOMPANY KAMALA ON HER LAST MEDICAL MISSION. SHE JOINS SOMMERVILLE IN 1937 BUT IN 1939, A HEALTH SCARE DISRUPTS HER EDUCATION.

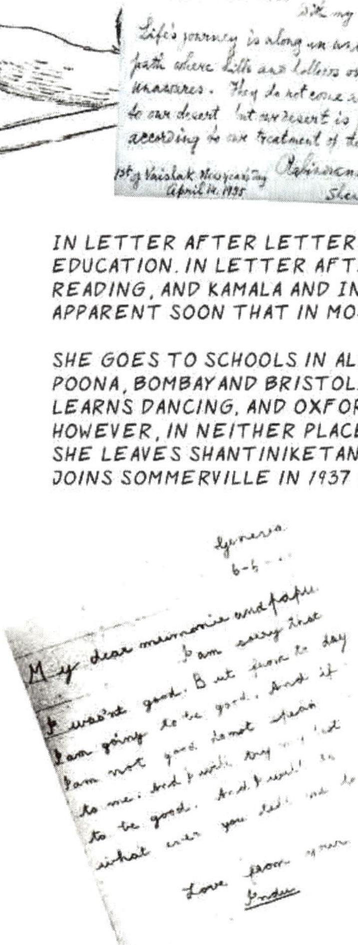

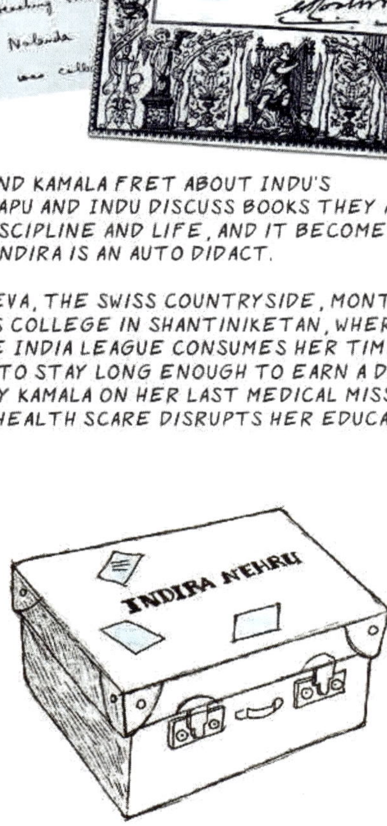

#SEVEN
YOU WILL LEARN TO LOOK DEATH IN THE EYE ONCE, TWICE, THRICE BEFORE YOU ARE EIGHTEEN.
FEBRUARY 1931 IS A MONTH OF GLOOM IN ANAND BHAWAN. ON THE 6TH, MOTILAL NEHRU PASSES AWAY, LEAVING THE FAMILY PLUNGED IN GRIEF. IT IS NOT AN UNTIMELY DEATH. THOSE ARE YET TO COME. BUT THE FIRST DEATH OF A BELOVED ONE IS A RITE OF PASSAGE.
WEEKS GO BY. INDIRA FINDS QUIET CORNERS TO BROOD IN. ON 27 FEBRUARY, AS SHE SITS IN THE VERANDAH READING A BOOK, SUDDENLY SHE HEARS SHOUTING.
BAM!
BAM!
CHANDRASHEKHAR AZAD, THE REVOLUTIONARY, IS MEETING AN ASSOCIATE, SUKHDEV. FORTY ARMED MEN HAVE BEEN SENT IN PURSUIT OF TWO. INDU HEARS GUNSHOTS IN THE DISTANCE.
The Leader
CHANDRASHEKHAR AZAD DEAD
UKHDEV CAPTURED
'I FELT NUMB, AS THOUGH I HAD BEEN DROPPED IN VERY HOT WATER OR VERY COLD WATER.'
A WOUNDED AZAD GIVES COVER TO HIS COMRADE-IN-ARMS, WHO MANAGES TO ESCAPE. AFTER A HALF-HOUR STANDOFF, AZAD SHOOTS HIMSELF. HE HAD ALWAYS MAINTAINED THAT HE WOULD NEVER BE CAPTURED ALIVE BY THE BRITISH.
LITTLE DID AZAD KNOW THAT A FEW KILOMETRES AWAY, A YOUNG GIRL WOULD LEARN A VITAL LESSON ABOUT THE LIFE OF PATRIOTS: IF YOU LOVE YOUR COUNTRY, YOU MUST ALSO BE READY TO DIE.

IN THE EARLY HOURS OF 28 FEBRUARY 1936, KAMALA NEHRU DIES IN SWITZERLAND.
AFTER MOURNING TOGETHER FOR A FEW DAYS, NEHRU RETURNS TO INDIA, TO THE TUMULT OF THE INDEPENDENCE MOVEMENT. INDIRA GOES TO ENGLAND, TO PREPARE FOR OXFORD. THE MEMORY OF HER MOTHER GASPING FOR BREATH IN THE BLACK FOREST WILL CLING TO HER.
IN THAT TIME, THERE WILL ONLY BE FEROZE.

4

IN WHICH WE GO TO ALLAHABAD

Whether it was because of his budding friendship with Rehaan or the fact that his grand-uncle had offered to drive them to Allahabad, since *he* was going there in his Innova taxi to hand over somebody's ashes to somebody for dispersion in the Sangam (so creepy!), Happy got himself included in the trip. Indira was intensely annoyed. She had looked forward to an interruption-free time with Piya didi and Miss Das. Rehaan, she still could tolerate, but Happy? Sigh, sigh, sigh. But it was barely a few days before school reopened, so the trip could only be now, or never.

'I don't know why you are complaining so much,' Arati scolded Indira. 'Here you get an all-expenses paid holiday with your divine Piya didi and your heroic Reema teacher—and you still find something to complain about? I, for one, am very happy that Happy's grand-uncle is taking you. Do you know what a helpful man Pal Singh is? When we had to rush to Safdarjung last year—who do you think sent us a taxi and did not take money for it?'

'Happy's grand-uncle,' said Indira, boredly.

'Exactly. They are such a fine family. When the fire happened, and I mentioned it to Navjot, Happy's mother, that our things were lying on the road, she immediately sent a taxi to pick them up and store them in their taxi-stand until we found a new room. You were in school, Nani. But Pal Singh himself came.'

'Fine,' Indira replied, resigned, though she continued to mutter under her breath. 'Pal dadaji might be nice and Navjot aunty is really sweet, but that Happy gets on my nerves,' she mumbled. 'I would never take him in my Vanar Sena.'

'What?' asked Arati. 'Stop muttering and finish packing.' A brand new red bag had been bought for the trip from the Wednesday market in their neighbourhood. 'I'll go and explain your medicines to Reema teacher.'

'Why?' asked Indira, mutinous again. 'I *know* what to take.'

'Am I your mother or are you my mother?' Arati asked. And that was that.

Gloomily, Indira began to take all her clothes out of the suitcase in which they were kept. There was no space for a cupboard in the room. It meant that every day the suitcase had to be rearranged. She liked her blue jeans and the matching t-shirt they had got for her birthday, and she liked the polka-dotted dress her mother's boss's niece had outgrown—but everything else was hateful. The mottled green kurta reminded her of frogs. The white flowy skirt her mother liked so much made her look shapeless like a cloud. She tried to pick the ones she hated the least.

Sardar Pal Singh turned out to be as quiet and wise as his grand-nephew was garrulous and foolish. He smiled at Indira shyly from under his long grey beard and luxurious moustache, and gave her a little pink cushion to make her more comfortable.

Rehaan sat up front with Pal Singh and all his gadgets—iPad, iPhone, Kindle, earphones and laptop. Miss Das and Piya didi sat in the middle, along with a dozen books about Indira Gandhi that Piya didi had insisted on carrying. Happy and Indira sprawled at the back. Indira was to have sat in the middle with Piya didi and Indira, but Happy refused to be alone with the ashes.

His grand-uncle scolded him in Punjabi for being such a coward. 'They are the ashes of a very good person,' he clarified. 'And you know what "Singh" means, don't you? It means lion!' But Happy was adamant. Indira said, 'Dadaji, I am not afraid. I'll sit in the back with him.' She was a little afraid, of course, but also felt a stab of compassion for Happy. At least for half-an-hour, he looked less cocky. Maybe she could make him a secondary member in her Vanar Sena?

It was a long drive, ten hours or so, made much longer by the many stops. Agra: to view the Taj Mahal, which Happy and Indira had never seen. ('Please, Pal Singhji,' begged Piya and Miss Das. 'The expressway takes us to Agra in only two hours, maybe we can take a detour for the sake of the kids?'). Mathura: to view the ghats that Piya simply had to photograph from thirty angles. Etawah: to stretch their legs and look for clean bathrooms. And several dhabas along the way because Rehaan and Happy complained of intense hunger every couple of hours.

Eventually the party reached the bed-and-breakfast in Allahabad's Lukerganj long past one in the morning. The three adults were exhausted; Happy and Indira, as bright-eyed and bouncy as they'd been at five in the morning, when they started travelling. They trooped into their dormitory, while Pal Singh went off to stay at his host's (a relative of the ashes).

The bed-and-breakfast had allotted to them a large room with bright yellow walls and white curtains, and five single beds with matching bedside tables. It opened into a little anteroom that had a large table with chairs all around. Most thoughtfully, there were two bathrooms instead of one, and the boys were quickly assigned the smaller one. For Indira, it was a little slice of heaven. She quickly memorized every detail of the room so she could tell Arati later—a painting of a mountain on the wall, a pattern of flowers in cross-stitch hung above her bed—while everyone took hot showers, changed into night-clothes and got into bed. Soon there were gentle snores from all but two (neighbouring) beds.

'Why aren't you asleep yet?' Piya didi whispered to Indira.

'I don't know,' Indira replied honestly. 'But I don't feel sleepy at all.'

'Are you missing Ma?'

Indira remained silent. She could hear Arati chatting with her, in her head, in a constant stream. 'Plait your hair before going to sleep or it will be all tangled in the morning.' 'Pull your sheet around yourself neatly.' 'Now, sleep. Okay?' Technically, was it missing someone if they seemed to travel right with you?

'Why are you awake, Piya didi?' Indira asked, turning on her side and raising her head on her elbow.

'I can't sleep if I haven't drawn something all day,' Piya confessed.

After a few minutes, she jumped up, took her large bag and

motioned for Indira to follow. Quietly, they made their way to the anteroom and as Indira watched, Piya's fingers deftly captured her face in a notebook, with a pencil. In fifteen minutes, a lovely likeness emerged. 'I'll colour it tomorrow,' Piya told Indira, 'and I shall gift it to your mother. Come, let's go to bed.'

The room was cold now, so very cold. Indira was unused to air-conditioning. Piya didi rooted in the cupboard, found a light dohaar and tucked her in. This time Indira fell asleep almost instantly, and was transported to the snowy mountains of the painting but through the night the white mountains resounded, peculiarly, with the soft sound of a pencil scratching on art paper.

At about eleven the next morning, the party was gathered in a little eatery called Netram Mulchand & Sons, a century-and-a-half-old sweet shop in Katra which was famous for its samosas and mithai. As they put away plate after plate, Rehaan asked Piya about all the places she would need to visit for the book.

'Swaraj Bhawan and Anand Bhawan, of course. We must start there.'

'I thought Indira Gandhi grew up in Anand Bhawan? What is Swaraj Bhawan?' Rehaan asked.

'What is now called Swaraj Bhawan was originally Anand Bhawan. That's where Indira Gandhi was born and spent her early years. It was a large mansion with forty-two rooms, gardens, an orchard, a riding ring, and a swimming pool that could be heated. Motilal Nehru loved to entertain in style. Scotch flowed richly every evening. He had a towering temper, by the way, which Jawaharlal inherited, and then Indira too. Afterwards, when the Nehrus turned to Satyagraha, everything changed. All the luxuries were given up.

'The house Indira was born into was much like the manor houses of British aristocrats—very Downton Abbeyesque. Difficult to maintain. In 1929, Motilal Nehru, the grand patriarch of the clan, started building a smaller house on the grounds. The old house was given to the Congress Party and rechristened Swaraj Bhawan. The new house was then passed on the old name, Anand Bhawan. Indira was always more attached to the old house, which had a central courtyard and wide corridors running all round it. But it was the new Anand Bhawan where she was married.'

A man overhearing the conversation chimed in, 'Yes. To Feroze Khan.'

'Not Khan. Feroze Gandhi. Though the family used to spell it Ghandy then.'

'No, madam, you don't know the details. She married Feroze Khan, a Muslim,' the man persisted.

'Parsi,' Piya said mildly. 'Most of the details about his life are quite well-established. He studied in Ewing Christian College; he went to prison several times.'

'And so what if he was Muslim?' Miss Das asked, a little belligerently.

'It would be better,' said the man. 'I am Muslim myself.'

Rehaan winked at her.

The waiter, who had been observing them with the corner of his eye and a cocked ear came over, ostensibly to clear the table. 'His real father was a Hindu, actually. Raj Bahadur Kamala Prasad Kakkar.'

'Now, *that*,' said Piya, 'might actually be true. Feroze Gandhi's biographer Bertil Falk acknowledges this rumour.'

'What's a bi-o-gra-pher?' asked Happy.

'A biographer is a person who writes about another person's life,' explained Rehaan.

'Then what is a person who *draws* another person's life?' Indira asked.

'You see, the word "graphy" originally came from a sense of drawing—because you drew characters. So I think biographer would be enough,' Piya said, doubtfully.

Everyone laughed. 'Swaraj Bhawan and Anand Bhawan.' Rehaan passed a small notebook to Indira. 'Make a list,' he instructed. 'Where else?'

'Ewing Christian College, where Feroze studied and where Indira and Feroze met for the first time. The old town, where the Nehrus used to live before Swaraj Bhawan.'

'You know, at breakfast, Mrs L was saying that one of her relatives, a Mrs Liddle, had rented out her house on Bank Road to Motilal Nehru for a while. We should go meet her.' Miss Das was the only member of the party who had woken up in time for breakfast and had managed to meet the lovely couple who ran the bed-and-breakfast.

'Write that down,' said Piya didi. 'Bank Road. Naini prison. Nehru wrote many of his letters to Indira from there. Later, she was imprisoned in Naini herself. Then Sangam, naturally. The place where the Ganga, Yamuna and the subterranean Saraswati meet, a super-holy place where the Kumbha Mela happens every twelve years.' She pushed her chair back and rose. 'Come on, let's hurry!'

Indira jumped up.

'Can we go back to the guest house and sleep while you do your research?' Rehaan asked, hesitantly.

'Yes, of course.'

'You mean, go to the guest house and watch the cricket match?' Miss Das glared.

'Maybe,' Rehaan grinned.

It was thus decided that the boys would go back to the guest house and establish contact with Pal Singh about going to the Sangam tomorrow, while Miss Das, Piya and Indira would complete their research at leisure. They would meet up in the evening outside the iconic A.H. Wheeler bookstore and compare notes.

An e-rickshaw was found and, finally, Indira got her two favouritest people all to herself.

'Civil Lines, bhaiya,' Piya instructed the e-rickshaw driver. 'Anand Bhawan.'

By dusk, Indira and Miss Das were exhausted. They had walked around Swaraj Bhawan and Anand Bhawan, in and out of its rooms and verandahs, so many times, that now they could navigate it in their sleep. Piya drew maps, took photos and made hundreds of little sketches—of a table here, a pelmet there, the curve of a stairway somewhere. 'Sorry, sorry,' she kept apologising, but dashed this way and that, pulled by invisible strings. Eventually the others gave up and sat outside the little store that sold books and allowed Piya to imagine the wedding Indira and Feroze had had, just outside Anand Bhawan, on her own.

'Did you know Eve Curie, the scientist Marie Curie's daughter, was a guest at the wedding? And Harivansh Rai Bachchan, the poet? He and his wife, Teji, sang a duet.' Piya had reappeared.

'Is that Amitabh Bachchan's father?' Indira asked, as they walked out of the gate together.

'Don't say that, darling.' Miss Das winced. 'Amitabh Bachchan is his son. They used to live in Allahabad. He was a professor at the university here.'

They jumped into another e-rickshaw and Piya told the driver to go to the old town, please. 'Chowk Mirganj.'

The rickshaw-walla looked shocked. 'Very congested, madam. Some parts are very, what shall I say, not honourable. Why do you want to go?'

'Please,' replied Piya.

They wound their way through the city, jumping over the many potholes, taking many turns, and entered the thickly populated part, with the trademark twinned beauty-and-ugliness of old Indian places, with narrow lanes upon which artistically painted rickshaws flitted about while cars remained stuck, shopkeepers and customers argued, and pig-tailed little girls smartly skirted piles of rubbish. 'Look,' Piya pointed out to Reema and Indira, 'See those old buildings. Aren't they beautiful?'

Indira looked up and was shocked.

'Those old buildings? But Piya didi, they are so dirty. They might fall on somebody's head!'

'Ah, but look at the symmetry, Indira. The jharokha work. The arches. The little overhanging verandahs.'

Miss Das rolled her eyes. 'It's insane, Piya. See how crowded the streets are. Carts and shops, pickle-sellers and jewellers, and a million people crowding about in the heat.'

'Yes,' Piya said, her voice soaked in bliss. 'It's perfect. This is where we'll set the scene. Let's park by that saree shop. I need to take some photographs. Come with me, Indira?'

'No need,' said Miss Das. 'She is tired.'

Piya didi crossed the road and, in a heartbeat, was lost in the crowds. For a moment, Indira felt bereft, even a little angry with Miss Das for not letting her go. But she did feel tired. Her heart was thumping. 'Don't worry,' said Miss Das, patting Indira's hand. 'She's off to 1942, the year of the Quit India movement. I think that's the year Indira and Feroze got married. Since it was an inter-religious marriage, there was a lot of opposition...'

'1942 was a long time ago,' Indira mused. 'People must have been quite against love marriages then.'

'Even now they are... if...' Miss Das trailed off, glaring at a gaggle of boys who were making a racket. 'Anyhow, Allahabad must have been much cleaner then! Heaven knows how your Piya didi is planning to set the scene here when the wedding was in Anand Bhawan. But don't ask me, ask her.'

GALLOOJI & SONS
I WONDER WHAT SHE WILL WEAR. I'M SURE IT'LL BE A BANARASI SAREE WITH REAL GOLD AND SILVER THREADS.
NO, NO! OF COURSE NOT. SHE'LL WEAR A KHADI SAREE THAT HER FATHER SPUN IN PRISON. NO BANARASI, AND NO GOLD. MY BANGLE-SELLER WENT TO ANAND BHAWAN YESTERDAY. SHE TOOK TWO HOURS TO CHOOSE GLASS BANGLES
SO BHAIYON, MODERNITY HAS COME TO ALLAHABAD AFTER ALL. A PURE-BRED KASHMIRI PANDIT IS MARRYING NOT ONLY OUTSIDE CASTE BUT OUTSIDE RELIGION?! TAUBA!
WHATEVER YOU SAY, BHAI, MY COUSIN WAS WITH FEROZE IN PRISON. SAID HE'S A WONDERFUL BOY, ALWAYS CRACKING JOKES. NOT HIGH-BORN OF COURSE. BUT THAT'S PROBABLY WHY HE HAS A NATURAL SYMPATHY FOR THE WORKING MAN
I HEARD PANDITJI ISN'T HAPPY WITH THIS MARRIAGE.
THAT'S EXPECTED, NO? HE HAD HIGH HOPES FOR HIS ONLY DAUGHTER.

UFF, DO YOU KNOW HOW MANY TIMES A DAY I'VE BEEN GOING TO ANAND BHAWAN IN THE LAST FEW WEEKS?! MY LEGS WILL FALL OFF.
THEY SAY FEROZE LOOKED AFTER KAMALAJI IN HER ILLNESS BETTER THAN ANY SON WOULD HAVE?
THEY ARE SO MODERN. WHERE DO YOU THINK THEY WILL GO FOR A HONEYMOON?
PRISON! DON'T YOU KNOW THINGS ARE GOING TO GET MUCH WORSE?

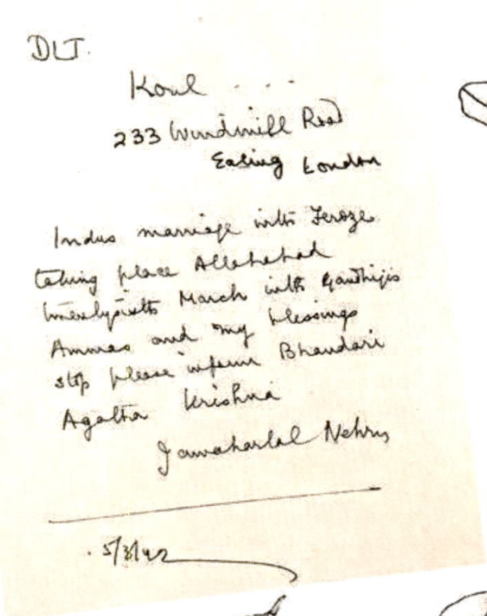

DLT.
Koul ...
233 Windmill Road
Ealing London

Indus marriage with Feroze taking place Allahabad twentysixth March with Gandhijis Ammas and my blessings stop please inform Bhandari Agatha Krishna

Jawaharlal Nehru

5/3/42

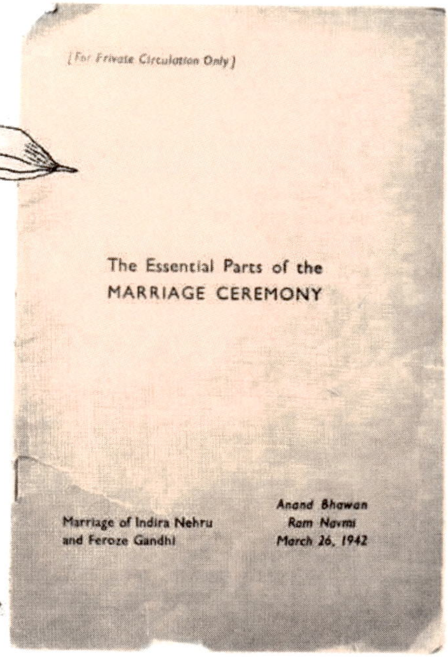

[For Private Circulation Only]

The Essential Parts of the
MARRIAGE CEREMONY

Marriage of Indira Nehru
and Feroze Gandhi

Anand Bhawan
Ram Navmi
March 26, 1942

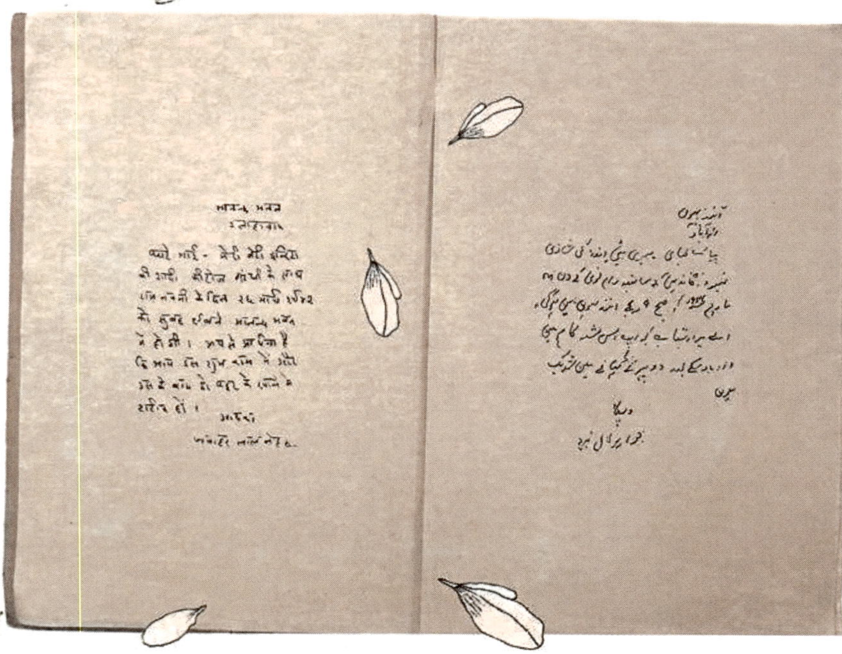

26 MARCH 1942, RAM NAVAMI, IS THE DATE SET FOR THE WEDDING. BAPU IS UNABLE TO ATTEND SINCE HE IS EN ROUTE TO DELHI, TO MEET SIR STAFFORD CRIPPS.

ON THE BACK PORCH OF ANAND BHAWAN, INDIRA AND FEROZE ARE MARRIED TO EACH OTHER IN A SYNCRETIC WEDDING CEREMONY.

IT IS NOT A MATCH THAT NEHRU EITHER DESIRES, OR QUITE SUPPORTS. HE HAD HIS OWN AMBITIONS FOR INDIRA AND FEELS RATHER LET DOWN THAT SHE WANTS TO SETTLE DOWN INTO MATRIMONY.

AFTER THE WEDDING, INDIRA AND FEROZE MOVE INTO A LITTLE RENTED PLACE, 5 FORT ROAD, IN ALLAHABAD, AND IN LATE MAY THEY GO TO KASHMIR FOR THEIR HONEYMOON. FROM GULMARG THEY SEND A TELEGRAM TO NEHRU.

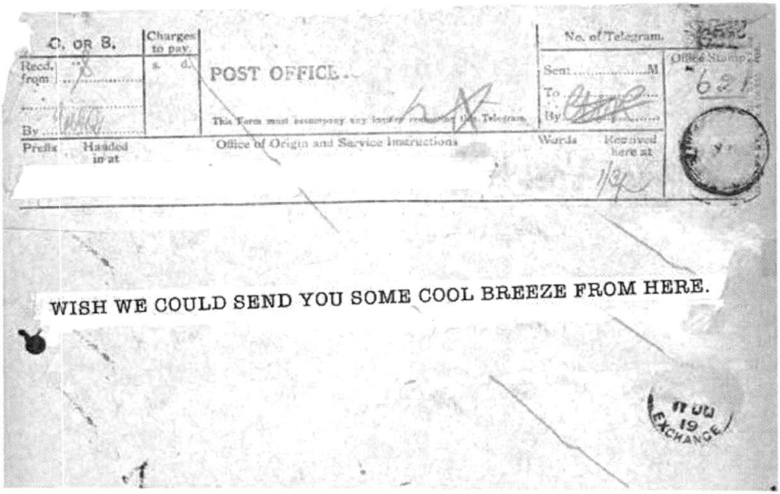

C. OR B.
Charges to pay
s. d.
Recd. from
By
Prefix Handed in at
POST OFFICE
This Form must accompany any inquiry respecting this Telegram.
Office of Origin and Service Instructions
No. of Telegram.
Sent ......M
To
By
Words Received here at
Office Stamp

WISH WE COULD SEND YOU SOME COOL BREEZE FROM HERE.

PAT COMES THE REPLY FROM THE PLAINS:

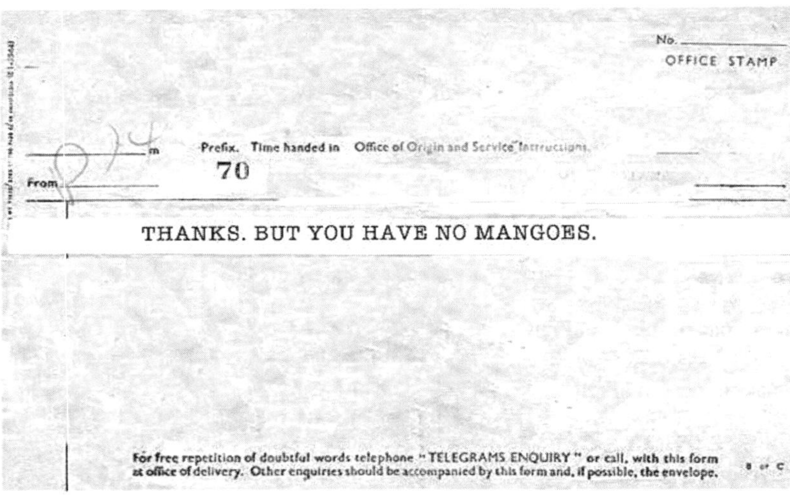

No.
OFFICE STAMP
Prefix. Time handed in Office of Origin and Service Instructions
From
70

THANKS. BUT YOU HAVE NO MANGOES.

For free repetition of doubtful words telephone "TELEGRAMS ENQUIRY" or call, with this form at office of delivery. Other enquiries should be accompanied by this form and, if possible, the envelope.

THE HONEYMOON IN KASHMIR IS PERHAPS THE SINGLE MOST PERFECT HOLIDAY OF INDIRA'S LIFE. THE MARRIAGE WOULD BE A STORMY ONE, WITH ACCUSATIONS AND SILENCES AND A TORMENTED SORT OF LOVE.

ON 8 AUGUST 1942, THE HISTORIC 'QUIT INDIA' RESOLUTION IS PASSED BY THE ALL INDIA CONGRESS COMMITTEE AT GOWALIA TANK IN BOMBAY. EARLY NEXT MORNING, NEHRU, WHO HAD MOVED THE RESOLUTION, IS ARRESTED AND SENT OFF TO JAIL FOR HIS LONGEST PRISON TERM YET.

A COUPLE OF DAYS LATER, BACK IN ALLAHABAD, AN ARREST WARRANT IS ISSUED FOR FEROZE. FOR A MONTH, HE MANAGES TO EVADE IT, STAYING UNDERGROUND AND MEETING INDIRA SECRETLY AT THE HOMES OF FRIENDS. BUT ON 11 SEPTEMBER, AT A FLAG HOISTING, BOTH ARE ARRESTED AND SENT OFF TO PRISON. FEROZE HAS BEEN IMPRISONED BEFORE; FOR INDU, IT IS A MUCH AWAITED MOMENT...

Naini Central Prison
Allahabad
25 March, 1943

Darling, darling Papu,

At last your letter has come – almost three weeks after it was written. But what is three weeks after a silence of seven months? I have been waiting and waiting and was finally giving up all hope of hearing from you. And all the time, miles away, you were waiting too. You behind one set of walls and I behind another. Is it funny or is it sad? I don't really know. ...

In the Female Ward (ghastly name!) our numbers are dwindling fast. Many have served their sentence and been released, convicted prisoners with longer sentences are transferred to other jails. We are missing some of them, especially those with children. For three months we had the most adorable baby – aged four to seven months. It was fascinating to watch her grow under our very eyes, making new noises, learning some new trick each day. While she was here I took her almost completely under my wing. She flourished on the schedule we drew up for her – sunbath, massage, orange juice, etc. Though this afforded much amusement for her mother and the other women, who thought it a huge joke that such a fuss be made over a mere baby – and a girl-child at that! ...

I haven't been reading anything special – there isn't anyone to send books. Had I known that I would be here for such a long time I might have made some arrangements. I have read a lot of old books – classical and otherwise, Balzac, Rousseau and so on – that one is always meaning to read but somehow keeps on postponing. Two new novels I liked. Phyllis Bottome's London Pride, the story of a little Cockney boy's courage during the Blitz. How well she writes! The second is Lin-Yu-tang's A Leaf in the Storm, which is the sequel to Moment in Peking. ... An altogether different kind of book which we all enjoyed was Verrier Elwin's detective story about the clouds, A Cloud that's Dragonish. Very fresh and light reading. ...

I seem to be ambling on and on. This is what comes of being "alone". – when one starts talking one doesn't know where to stop. Write soon. Write often. Tell me about yourself. How is your arm? The one that was worrying you in Dehra. I hope it doesn't pain or trouble you any more, and that you are looking after it and the rest of yourself too.

Lots and lots of love to you,
Indu

AND IF PRISON IS ONE RITE OF PASSAGE, THE OTHER IS MOTHERHOOD.

Ahmadnagar Fort Prison
21 August, 1944

Darling,
So you have made me a grandfather!
I received the message yesterday in the afternoon. It had apparently come by telephone. I felt very happy that this tension was over and that you had successfully launched into motherhood. Pantji managed somehow to produce some very good and fresh peras at teatime to celebrate the occasion. I hope it is well with you and the little one. All our friends here send both of you their love and blessings.
All my love,
Your loving,
Papu

THE NEWBORN'S NAME IS A MOUTHFUL: RAJIVA RATNA BIRJEES NEHRU GANDHI. HE IS A SUNNY HANDSOME BABY. TWO YEARS AND THREE MONTHS LATER, ON 14 DECEMBER 1946, RAJIV ACQUIRES A BABY BROTHER, AFTER A COMPLICATED LABOUR THAT NEARLY KILLS INDIRA. BY THEN, NEHRU IS THE HEAD OF THE INTERIM GOVERNMENT IN NEW DELHI.

ON 15 AUGUST 1947, INDIA BECOMES AN INDEPENDENT NATION AND JAWAHARLAL NEHRU, THE FIRST PRIME MINISTER.

5

IN WHICH PAL SINGH TELLS A STORY

On the way back from Allahabad, everybody was in a bad mood. Happy and Indira were despondent that the best-holiday-ever would soon end, and in an effort to deal with that sinking sensation, they sniped at each other constantly.

Whatever Indira said, Happy felt an intense need to repeat. Say, they were passing by a pretty-looking fort in the distance and she said, 'Wow, that's so beautiful.' Happy would immediately repeat, in a shrill falsetto, 'Woooooow, thaaaaat's sooooooo beauuuuutifullllll.' Just that. But over and over and over again until Indira wanted to hurl him out of the Innova. Her greatest regret was that yesterday, in a sudden burst of friendship, she had confided to Happy her plan to start her own Vanar Sena, and worse, even offered him a sort of generalship. Damn.

Miss Das and Rehaan, while seated next to each other, were not on speaking terms. Nobody knew why. But it had begun over a difference of opinion about the right way to make scrambled eggs, during their visit to Naini Prison.

Piya, sitting next to Pal Singh, was in a sort of a trance. Every now and then she would fish out a notebook and scribble in it obsessively.

Finally, after lunch, when the silence became too oppressive even for him, Pal Singh asked Piya about the mysterious book she was writing. After she had explained the basic idea, he began to speak in his slow, gravelly voice:

'I know you came to see Allahabad and understand the place where Indiraji was born. I can tell you something about the day she died—was killed. At the time, I was still a young man and had come to

Delhi only recently with another boy from my village, a close friend, Balwant. My friend had a relative who owned a taxi stand near Khan Market. Both of us started working for him. Our maalik's family also owned a car repair shop in Prithviraj Market and, at night, we used to sleep in a little room above the repair shop. Our taxis were often hired by government departments, and we used to drive politicians, take them here and there. Twice, I saw Indira Gandhi. She used to walk very fast.

'It was a good life for a young man. I had no wife or children then, and whatever money I sent home was appreciated by the family. I drove an Ambassador. It was the main car in those days. A few Marutis had come out earlier that year. A few imported cars were spotted here and there. All the embassies had their big cars. But otherwise, the Ambassador was the queen of the streets and Delhi was a quiet, simple place. Not like now. So much traffic, so many cars. We used to feel really special those days, driving cars.

'On 31 October, we were at the stand when rumours began to circulate that Bibi had been shot by Sardars. No one knew then that they were her own guards. Business was slow that day, so we just stayed put at the shop. By late afternoon, we started to hear that buses were being stopped near AIIMS and Sardars were dragged out—but we didn't really pay attention. At night, though, things got grim. We turned off the lights in our little room and remained in the dark. We stayed up, vigilant, and all night we heard groups of people coming to loot the expensive shops owned by Sardars in Khan Market. Trucks were filled with things and taken away in the night.

'Next morning, the other shopkeepers in that area, mostly Hindus, who were worried about what they were hearing, told us to go home; basically, go to our maalik's house in Gautam Nagar. We got into our taxi and rushed that way. At INA market, there was a mob. We raced past. Vehicles were burning. In the distance, you could see columns of smoke rising.'

'That area—near Green Park? Wasn't it horribly afflicted by the riots?' Piya asked softly.

'Yes. But our lane in Gautam Nagar was mostly full of Sikhs, and the families got all their lathis and weapons out. Many Hindu neighbours offered to hide the young men and boys. Gautam Nagar remained relatively unscathed. A few people did shave their hair and beards to save their lives—I don't judge them harshly for it. But I wouldn't have done it myself.

'The next day we got a job. Violence was escalating in places like Trilokpuri, a few local Congress politicians were planning riots, and the police, where they were not complicit, were turning a blind eye, though we only learnt of this later. Have you heard the name of Hari Krishna Shastri? He was Lal Bahadur Shastri's son and a senior Congress politician. His office used to rent taxis from our stand. He managed to send a message that he needed a taxi to drop a guest of his to Rajasthan, somewhere near Udaipur. My maalik asked the two of us to go. Early in the morning, we got to Hari Krishna Shastri's house in Janpath. He himself came down to see his guest off. His secretary gave us a small red light, saying that as long as we had it, nobody would try to stop us.

'We left. The roads were comparatively empty at that hour and we drove straight down to Udaipur, stopping only when the guest asked us to. We finally dropped him off in the early evening. Then, after freshening up, we started the long drive back, without the red light of course, since there was no VIP in the taxi anymore. We were exhausted by then.

'We drove and drove and drove, and by the time we came to a dhaba and decided to stop for dinner, it was pitch dark. We were young in those days and when we got hungry, we felt we could eat a house. At the dhaba we went up to the counter and asked for parathas and butter chicken. Back then, I used to eat non-veg. Now, for many years, I only eat veg. Once we'd placed the order, we heard a man say loudly from behind us, "After killing our mother, you now want to eat butter chicken?" For a second, I didn't even understand what was going on. My friend replied, quite calmly, "Have only two Sardars been born in this country, bhai? We are from Himachal, not even from Punjab, where all the troubles are happening." The muttering continued as we paid and walked to a table and sat down.

'The dhaba owner tried to make nice. He sent a young fellow to give us water and clear the table. From the corner of my eye, I kept watching that group of men. Their numbers were swelling consistently. I pointed it out to my friend. "Do you think they might turn on us?"

'"I curse this Beant Singh and Satwant Singh," my friend replied angrily. "They've reduced us to this. Constantly making us look over our shoulders."

'"Look," I told him, "we should get out of here now, while we can."

'Quietly we walked to our taxi, without eating. We hoped to slip away unnoticed but the boy who had brought our food started shouting, "Where did the Sardarjis go? Where did the Sardarjis go?"

'The men saw us getting into our taxi, and we knew immediately that we were in trouble. For a second nothing happened. Then the men rushed out to follow us. We reversed our taxi and got out of there. But soon it became clear that the men had motorcycles and a car, and were following us. We went like the wind, but the men persisted. They were locals; we were outsiders. It was their territory. At one point, we decided to go off the highway and turned into a kachha road. My friend stopped the vehicle and I went back and broke the tail lights of our taxi.'

'Why?' asked Miss Das, in a small voice from the back.

'So only the headlights would glow, showing the way ahead to the driver. But if someone were following, they wouldn't be able to see the car,' Rehaan replied, in an equally small voice.

'Jee,' said Pal Singh. 'Exactly. We just ran the car through those narrow broken inside roads and by the time we hit the highway again, we had shaken the men off our trail. But a strange fear persisted. Petrol was also running low but we didn't want to stop the taxi anywhere. It was late night by now and we couldn't trust anyone anymore. Somehow or the other, almost on fumes, we reached the outskirts of Jaipur and found a petrol pump. There was a large repair shop adjoining the pump. It was nearly 2 a.m. The name of the shop was written in Hindi, English and Gurumukhi. We jangled the shutter and spoke in Punjabi. The old Sardar himself had stayed on in the shop that night. His workshop was huge, and he welcomed us warmly.

'We parked in a corner of the workshop, freshened up, drank some water and went to sleep. Next morning, the old man woke us up and fed us parathas. He gave us petrol and repaired our tail lights, all for free. Then he told us that, to be safe, we should not drive to Delhi by ourselves. Instead, he would hook us up with a friend in Kotputli. They would get us five or six passengers to Delhi, and we should charge a small sum from them. If they were with us, nobody would harm us.

'At the time, we did not question his advice. We just did what he said. We needed to get back to Delhi, one way or the other. And we did.

'By the time we entered the city, the army had been called in and the madness had subsided, as though by magic.'

Indira and Happy were listening intently. They had a hundred questions, but didn't know where to start.

'What did you do next, Pal Singhji?' Miss Das asked.

'Oh, I can't remember exactly. But within a few weeks, elections were declared. Hari Krishna Shastri, Lal Bahadur Shastri's son, contested from Fatehpur in UP. Do you know Fatehpur? It's ahead of Kanpur. My friend and I were hired for his campaign. For two whole months we stayed in UP, driving him everywhere. Even when he went to give speeches or to people's houses, asking for their votes. He won the elections, became an MP, and gave us both a reward. That was a happy time.'

Pal Singh slowed the car to a halt. 'Here. You must be hungry now? This dhaba is very good. Why don't you all eat here? There are clean bathrooms too. We have a relative who lives close by. Happy and I will just go visit them.'

Happy didn't particularly want to go with his grand-uncle to meet some boring relative, but there appeared to be no choice, not now. So he went.

The rest of the party was subdued. Eventually, after the buttery parathas and dal makhani had warmed them up, Miss Das said, 'Indira, what Pal Singhji told us, now that was oral history.'

Rehaan said, 'Can you put this story in your book, Piya?'

'I don't know,' Piya said. 'It depends on the shape the book takes finally. And books have their own minds. But it's really ironical, you know?'

'Ironic,' corrected Miss Das.

Piya took no notice. 'Once in 1947, when all these riots were happening in Delhi after Partition, Mrs Gandhi was returning from the refugee camps where she had been volunteering, and she found a crowd following a single man. She asked the driver to stop the car, but he refused to. He slowed down somewhat and Mrs Gandhi streaked out, barefoot, and put herself between the solitary man and the crowd.

'"What do you think you are doing?" they asked.

'"I am saving this man's life; you can kill him only after you kill me," she replied.

'"Do you think we can't kill you?"

'"Anybody can kill me, but you are not going to..." she replied.

'And to think of the violence that happened in her name.'

They ate in silence.

'How old was she in 1947?' Rehaan asked.

Indira replied quickly, 'Thirty. She was born in 1917.'

'Well done!' said Miss Das.

Rehaan, meanwhile, was turning the pages of Piya's notebook, pausing at the sketches she had made. 'I am now getting really interested in this book, Piya. Somehow the complexity of her story gets overshadowed by talk of the Emergency and Operation Blue Star...wait, what are all these post-its?' he asked, intrigued at the vast number of yellow squares fluttering like little flags.

'When I plan a chapter I just scribble possible images on post-its. It's only much later that I turn them into full chapters. Basically, these post-its are my graphic notes. Full disclosure, I just leave them here and there. Reema, while OCDing, rescues them and sticks them here.'

'Can I see it?' Indira asked.

'May,' corrected Miss Das automatically.

'May I see it, Miss,' they all repeated.

'I am going to look for a toilet,' Miss Das said huffily and got up to leave. Rehaan followed her, pretending he was going to smoke.

SEPTEMBER 1947: THE HORRORS OF PARTITION ARE VISITED UPON THE CAPITAL. INDIRA WORKS TIRELESSLY IN THE REFUGEE CAMPS.

29 JANUARY 1948: THE DAY BEFORE MAHATMA GANDHI IS SHOT, INDIRA AND RAJIV GO TO VISIT HIM, ALONG WITH SAROJINI NAIDU.

2 AUGUST 1948: JAWAHARLAL NEHRU MOVES FORMALLY TO TEEN MURTI HOUSE, AND INDIRA BECOMES HIS OFFICIAL HOSTESS. SHE SHUTTLES BETWEEN LUCKNOW, WHERE FEROZE LIVES AND WORKS, AND DELHI.

1951–52: BEFORE INDEPENDENT INDIA'S FIRST GENERAL ELECTIONS, INDIRA CAMPAIGNS FOR FEROZE AS WELL AS FOR NEHRU. FEROZE WINS AND, OVER THE YEARS, TAKES ON THE ROLE OF THE OPPOSITION IN PARLIAMENT, MUCH TO NEHRU'S CHAGRIN.

2 FEBRUARY 1959: INDIRA IS ELECTED PRESIDENT OF THE CONGRESS PARTY. ALLEGEDLY, IN HER TIME AS THE PRESIDENT, SHE ADVISES NEHRU TO DISMISS THE COMMUNIST GOVERNMENT LED BY EMS NAMBOODIRIPAD IN KERALA.

JUNE 1960: AFTER A DECADE OF STORMS AND SILENCES IN THEIR MARRIAGE, FEROZE AND INDIRA RECONCILE AFTER HIS HEART ATTACKS AND SPEND AN IDYLLIC HOLIDAY IN KASHMIR WITH THE BOYS. SHE DECIDES THAT AFTER NEHRU, SHE WOULD DEVOTE HERSELF TO FEROZE'S CAREER.

8 SEPTEMBER 1960: FEROZE GANDHI PASSES AWAY AFTER A MASSIVE HEART ATTACK.

19 NOVEMBER 1962: ON HER 45TH BIRTHDAY, SHE FLIES TO TEZPUR WITH RED CROSS SUPPLIES FOR SOLDIERS EVEN AS THE CHINESE OCCUPY 50,000 SQUARE MILES OF INDIAN TERRITORY.

24 JANUARY 1966: INDIRA IS SWORN IN AS THE PRIME MINISTER OF INDIA.

MARCH 1966: MRS GANDHI VISITS THE UNITED STATES AND PRESIDENT LYNDON B. JOHNSON IS SO CHARMED BY HER THAT HE STAYS ON, UNINVITED, TO DINNER AT THE INDIAN AMBASSADOR'S HOUSE.

UNFORTUNATELY, AMERICAN WHEAT, FOR WHICH INDIA IS DESPERATE, REMAINS AS ELUSIVE AS IT HAD IN THE PAST. ALTHOUGH MRS GANDHI SWALLOWS HER PRIDE AND DEVALUES THE RUPEE AS A BITTER CONCESSION TO THE IMF, WHEN THE 'AID' REMAINS ERRATIC, THE FAMOUS NEHRU TEMPER UNCOILS ITSELF. MRS GANDHI DECIDES UPON TWO THINGS. INDIA WILL INTENSIFY ITS NON-ALIGNMENT AND WILL ATTAIN FOOD SECURITY AT ANY COST.

IN THE ELECTIONS OF 1966–67, MRS GANDHI EMERGES AS AN EXTREMELY POPULAR MASS LEADER. NO LONGER IS SHE THE 'GOONGI GUDIA' DR RAM MANOHAR LOHIA HAD ONCE DESCRIBED HER AS.

ON 25 FEBRUARY 1968, INDIRA BECOMES A MOTHER-IN-LAW, WHEN HER ELDER SON, RAJIV, MARRIES SONIA MAINO.

21 SEPTEMBER 1968: INDIRA GANDHI SPLITS THE INTELLIGENCE BUREAU TO CREATE A SEPARATE EXTERNAL INTELLIGENCE WING CALLED RESEARCH AND ANALYSIS WING (R&AW), BOTH REPORTING DIRECTLY TO THE PMO.

20 JULY 1969: 14 INDIAN BANKS ARE NATIONALIZED BY PRESIDENTIAL ORDINANCE. THERE IS WIDESPREAD REJOICING BECAUSE IT IS FELT THAT THE POOR NOW HAVE ACCESS TO THE NATION'S BANKS!

12 NOVEMBER 1969: INDIRA GANDHI IS EXPELLED BY THE CONGRESS, WHICH TRIED HER 'IN ABSENTIA'. THIS LEADS TO THE FIRST SPLIT IN THE CONGRESS.

HOWEVER, THE CONGRESS (O)'S NO-CONFIDENCE MOTION AGAINST THE GOVERNMENT, LED BY MORARJI DESAI, IS DEFEATED, AND INDIRA GANDHI'S CONGRESS (R) REMAINS IN POWER WITH THE SUPPORT OF THE COMMUNIST PARTY AND THE AKALI DAL.

NOVEMBER 1970: A LETTER OF INTENT IS GIVEN TO SANJAY GANDHI, INDIRA'S YOUNGER SON, WHO DREAMS OF BUILDING AN INDIGENOUS CAR. THE GRANTING OF THIS LICENCE IS HEAVILY CRITICIZED IN PARLIAMENT BY OPPOSITION LEADERS.

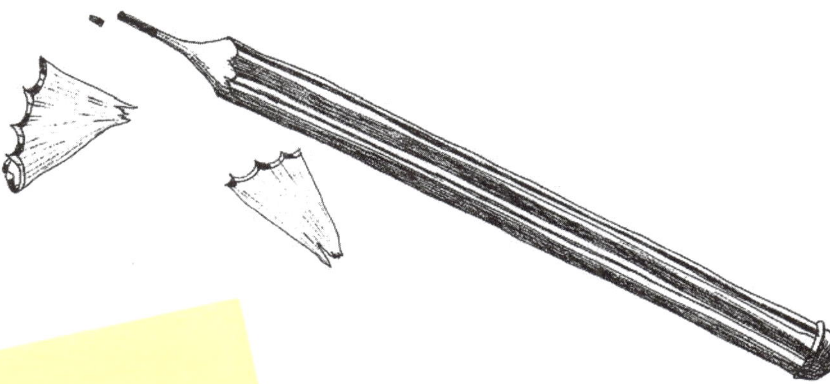

LATE 1960S:
GREEN REVOLUTION

6

IN WHICH WE HEAR A WAR STORY

On Sundays, Arati did not go in to work. It was for this one luxury alone, a whole day to herself and her daughter, that she turned down full-time positions which might have come with living quarters. Full-time positions, even with the most benevolent of employers, encroached upon boundaries all the time—there were always guests coming over and emergency baby-sitting to do, and Madam not wanting to leave dirty bartans in the sink overnight.

On her sacred Sundays, Arati slept in and made herself two or three cups of luxuriously boiled masala chai before she embarked on other errands, well past eight o'clock. This morning, though, at half-past seven, mother and daughter were standing at the bus stop, fanning themselves with folded newspapers. They had left home early to get to the suburbs before the day got hot and dry, but even at this early hour their faces had become red in the sun. A week had passed after Indira's return from Allahabad and though she still had one or two fresh anecdotes that Arati had not yet heard more than ten times, she no longer talked non-stop about the trip.

'Uff, you and your Reema teacher,' Arati said, half-proud and half-exasperated. 'All the strange homework she gives! Why Indira? Arre baba, your grandfather liked Indira Gandhi and after boys, boys, boys in the family, when you were born, he said we should name you Indira. Your father and I liked the name. So we said fine. Plus, you know nobody can argue with your Dadaji.'

'But Piya didi said...'

'And as though Reema teacher was not enough, now there is Piya didi!'

'Ma, Piya didi said this is "oral history". And the main thing is, when I ask Dadaji all these questions and complete the project, she might include my story in her book.'

'I thought she's an artist? You're saying she's a writer now.'

The bus had rolled up and they quickly got in. It was one of those beautiful red buses, long sleek body and air-conditioned inside. Though the tickets were expensive, Arati gave in to the holiday mood and did not grumble.

'She *is* an artist. An amazing artist, Ma. There are all these drawings in their house. The book is words plus pictures. It's called a graphic biography.'

The conductor arrived, and Indira's stream of chatter was interrupted again.

'Two tickets to Safdarjung,' Arati said.

'Hospital?' he asked, printing out the stubs.

Arati smiled. 'Not today.' Indira looked studiously outside.

'Oh,' said the conductor, sticking his (unnecessary) pen behind his ear, even as he took great delight in sticking his (stubby) nose into their affairs. 'Where then?'

'Oh, just to visit my in-laws,' Arati replied. 'We'll take the metro from Safdarjung.'

Fortunately, right then, the bus nearly collided with a motorbike and the conductor rushed up front to fight.

'Haan,' said Arati, poking Indira. 'So, your Piya didi doesn't have a job?'

'Ma,' Indira said defensively, 'writing and painting are jobs. You just don't go to an office or a school at a fixed time.'

Arati didn't say anything more. She closed her eyes, and in five minutes she was fast asleep. Indira watched the city pass her by, the houses and shops and trees melding into each other. The large sleek cars jostling with nimble bicycles and busy-bee autos, and every surface burning up in the heat. She felt an ache in her chest that was pleasant and unfamiliar. When she grew up she would know this feeling—it was home-love, the love of a specific place—but for the moment, she settled on day-dreaming. One day she would drive a red

Nano down these familiar streets, wearing Ray Ban sunglasses and a steel-faced watch. She would straighten her hair and carry a thin, silver laptop, like M, to office.

After the air-conditioned bus, the metro. 'How expensive the tickets have become, Nani!' Arati exclaimed. Then a little van and, finally, into the territory of narrow streets and exposed-brick houses, a shared Vikram.

Perspiring heavily, they were finally home!

Arati's in-laws, Indira's grandparents, had built a little house on a tiny plot of land they had bought with the money Dhol Bahadur Thapa got when he retired from the army. He could have got a larger parcel of land and been able to afford a better locality if he had sold the property in Gulmi, but that he held on to, for his sons. This was a single-storey house with two large rooms, a kitchen and a bathroom which Dadaji had tiled himself. There was a little strip of land outside where Dadi grew vegetables and put out pickles, and a tiny strip at the back where Dadaji had planted a neem tree, which was now as high as the house.

Arati and her mother-in-law parked themselves on the bed inside and started to exchange gossip about their entire extended clan, who were scattered across India, with a few strands in Nepal.

After lunch, Indira went and sat down next to Dadaji, on the mat in the outside room, and began to explain the whole oral history project. 'I need to know why you named me Indira.'

'After the prime minister, Mrs Gandhi, Nani. You know that. Everyone knows that.'

'But why?'

'What kind of a question is that?'

It was not an easy exercise. Indira's grandfather was usually a quiet man, and showed his affection through smiles and gentle gestures rather than words and long family stories—her Dadi was good at that. But Indira persevered. And persevered. Then some more.

Finally, Dadaji opened up.

'To explain why I respect Indira Gandhi so much, we have to go back to the story of 1962, Nani. At the time, she was not a minister or anything. She was just Panditji's daughter.'

'Wasn't there a war in 1962?'

'Yes, you know India has fought four major wars. 1962 was against China—and that war we lost. And then against Pakistan, in 1965, 1971 and 1999. We Gorkhas fought bravely in all of them, and after 1962, we haven't lost any wars. In 1962, Nani, I was a very young man. A new soldier.'

'What is war like?'

'Eh, you ask questions like those TV journalists, Nani,' he laughed and patted her on the cheek. 'Now I know why your mother spends so much on your education instead of saving for your dowry. What is war like? Hmm...' Dadaji closed his eyes and continued, 'Time moves very quickly. Then very slowly. Then very quickly again.'

'Stop, Dadu,' she said. She quickly got her mother's phone from the next room and started recording what he said.

Dadaji laughed.

'So,' Indira prompted. 'I asked you what war is like. You said, time moves very quickly. Then very slowly. Then very quickly again...'

'There is the smell of exploding gunpowder. It really hits you. There is the sound of gun shots. There are the cries of wounded soldiers. You would think your heart would go dhak-dhak-dhak loudly. But it doesn't; you are calm; your heart behaves itself. Then suddenly you hear the cry, "Aayo Gorkhaali", and your blood rushes to your head. You feel so brave, as though nothing can stop you and no bullet can pierce your skull.'

Dadaji fell silent.

'So, 1962,' prompted Indira.

'I had just joined the First Battalion of the Ninth Gorkha Rifles. I still remember the train ride, Nani, from Gulmi to Dehradun. I was so thrilled. After a brief training, we were deployed to a remote place in Eastern India. Tawang. And, almost immediately, we got sucked up in war fever. Initially it was all a haze. We were instructed to prepare for the Chinese. I remember walking for at least five days before we came up to a mountain we had been told to defend. I remember the cold nights. Our clothing seemed inadequate, and I was always hungry.'

'Hungry?'

'Yes. Then, one day, in an army helicopter she arrived.'

'Indira Gandhi?'

'Indira Gandhi. All the politicians were afraid to come, you see. The Chinese were right there and there was the serious threat of Assam getting captured. But there she was, striding towards us that morning. A little lady, thin and determined. She was not in politics then. From Guwahati, she flew to Tezpur, and then came to us. Our Platoon Commander came to greet her. She said she had brought food, blankets, medicines, warm clothes. And that she should be given a list of what we required. She would go back to Delhi and arrange for more provisions. Our commander introduced us individually to her, and she chatted for a few moments with each of us. She kept saying we were only a little older than her boys and the whole country appreciated what we were doing; she was so proud of us. She came back again, as promised, with more supplies. But that day the Commander did not let her chit-chat with us, and sent her back with folded hands as soon as he could. We had looked forward to her return visit so much that we were a little disappointed. The very next day, the Chinese came.'

Dadi came into the room with a large glass of tea for Dadaji and nimbu paani for Indira. 'Chatter, chatter, chatter. No rest, you two!'

As soon as she had gone back inside, Indira turned to Dadaji.

'Then what happened?'

'They came in large numbers, Nani, and there was confusion everywhere when the fight started. We had always been told, "A Gorkha does not retreat. He goes down fighting. He never retreats." It was the saddest and most shameful day of our lives when we were forced to abandon our position. But we had no choice. I remember the bombs all around us; we were outnumbered. There were dead soldiers on the battlefield. They seemed to have better fire than us, and my platoon commander shouted over the noise, asking us to withdraw. That mountain still haunts me.'

'So we lost that war?'

'We did. And they say Panditji never recovered from the shock. He had always been friendly to the Chinese. After that loss, though, we really got our house in order. And years later, under Indira

Gandhi's leadership, we won the 1971 war, which healed a few of the memories of '62. My battalion did not fight in that war. But my cousin, Shyam Gurung, also from Gulmi, fought and even won a medal for bravery!'

'Did you ever meet Indira Gandhi after that?'

'We saw her once afterwards. When we were visiting your Dadi's younger brother in Allahabad, her home town, we went to a rally where she addressed everyone. She was the prime minister then. But she would lose that election. People did not like the Emergency. We also saw Panditji's house in Allahabad. It was a nice museum. But that image of her in 1962—in a saree and a military coat, walking determinedly towards us in Tawang—that stayed in my mind. I decided then that when I had a daughter, I would call her Indira.'

Unknown to Indira, her grandmother and mother had also been listening to the stories from the kitchen, where they were cooking together. Now they came out and joined them, and her Dadi said, 'But we never had daughters. I had three boys, your father and uncles. And then your uncles had only sons. So when you were born, finally your Dadaji got his wish. We named you Indira.'

'And now,' said Arati, 'you'd better get ready. We have a long way to go. Dadi has packed dinner for us.'

All through the next day, Indira composed the story of her name in her notebook. She wrote about the war that was lost, and ended with the war that was won. She made a fair copy of the essay, walked down to the cyber café, and emailed the two-page scan to Piya didi. Piya didi had said she might go to her grandmother's house in the hills for the rest of the summer. But she had promised to write.

29 APRIL–22 JULY 1970, CAMBODIA.
THE VIETNAM WAR EXTENDS TO EASTERN CAMBODIA AS THE US MILITARY TRIES TO FLUSH OUT THE RESISTANCE FIGHTERS OF THE VIET CONG.
SEPTEMBER 1970, INDIA.
INDIRA GANDHI BRINGS AN AMENDMENT TO ABOLISH THE TAX-FREE PRIVY PURSES (AND VARIOUS ATTENDANT PERKS) WHICH HAD BEEN GRANTED TO FORMER PRINCES IN INDIA IN 1947 AND COST THE EXCHEQUER SOME 60 MILLION DOLLARS.
12/13 NOVEMBER 1970, EAST PAKISTAN.
AT NIGHT, WHILE THE LOCAL POPULATION SLEEPS, A DEADLY TROPICAL CYCLONE HITS THE FUNNEL-SHAPED COASTLINE.
THE MAINLAND HEARS OF THE TRAGEDY MUCH LATER.

THE PAKISTAN ADMINISTRATION AND GENERAL AGHA MUHAMMAD YAHYA KHAN, PRESIDENT AND COMMANDER-IN-CHIEF, EVENTUALLY WAKE UP TO THE TRAGEDY.
MRS GANDHI IS OFFERING US 50 RELIEF HELICOPTERS ... PRESIDENT NIXON GAVE ONLY 12 ...
CAN'T ACCEPT! OUR SECURITY WILL BE THREATENED.
SIR, WHY DID THE GOVERNMENT NOT PROVIDE ANY FLOOD CONTROL SYSTEM?
LOOK, I'M TRULY SORRY ABOUT THE CYCLONE. BUT WE ARE IN THE HANDS OF ALLAH. WHO CAN STOP A CYCLONE?
THESE ANTI-NATIONAL BINGOS! EVEN A CYCLONE IS A PUNJABI CONSPIRACY!

THE BHOLA CYCLONE, WHICH KILLS 500,000 EAST PAKISTANIS, FURTHER DAMAGES THE FRACTIOUS RELATIONSHIP BETWEEN THE TWO HALVES OF PAKISTAN THAT LIE ON EITHER SIDE OF INDIA.
WEST PAKISTAN CONTROLS ADMINISTRATION, POLICY-MAKING, COMMERCE AND THE ARMY. WHILE THE MORE POPULOUS EAST PAKISTAN, THE RICE BOWL, IS TREATED ALMOST LIKE AN OUTPOST OF THE EMPIRE. IN FACT, THE FIRST CRACKS IN THE RELATIONSHIP BETWEEN WEST PAKISTAN AND EAST PAKISTAN HAD SURFACED AS EARLY AS 1948, EVEN BEFORE THE HIGH OF INDEPENDENCE HAD SUBSIDED.
EAST PAKISTAN
INDIA
HEY! HOW WAS YOUR TRIP TO THE EAST?
SO BACKWARD THESE BINGOS ARE. ROADS, INFRASTRUCTURE – RUBBISH!
NOW, WHOSE FAULT IS THAT?
1948, DHAKA.
LET ME MAKE IT VERY CLEAR TO YOU. THE STATE LANGUAGE OF PAKISTAN IS GOING TO BE URDU AND NO OTHER LANGUAGE. AND ANYONE WHO TRIES TO MISLEAD YOU IS REALLY THE ENEMY OF PAKISTAN.
NO, WE DO NOT AGREE!

TWO DECADES ON, THE FACE OF EAST PAKISTAN POLITICS IS THE DYNAMIC BENGALI LEADER, SHEIKH MUJIBUR RAHMAN. HIS SIX-POINT PROGRAMME (FORMULATED IN 1966), WHICH DEMANDS COMPLETE AUTONOMY FOR EAST PAKISTAN IN ALL MATTERS EXCEPT DEFENCE AND FOREIGN POLICY, BECOMES THE CORNERSTONE OF A NEW RADICAL MOVEMENT.
IN DECEMBER 1970, PAKISTAN CONDUCTS ITS FIRST FREE AND FAIR DEMOCRATIC ELECTIONS BASED ON UNIVERSAL ADULT SUFFRAGE. EAST PAKISTANIS GIVE THEIR BELOVED MUJIB'S AWAMI LEAGUE A THUMPING VICTORY.
WHO THE HELL DOES YOUR ANALYSIS? AWAMI HAS GOT 160 SEATS IN EAST PAKISTAN. MUJIB HAS GOT A CLEAR MAJORITY!
THE PAKISTAN OBSERVER
Landslide victory for AL
MUJIBUBAGS BOTH SEATS : NURUL AMIN LEADING
Peaceful bolling in the city
THE NEXT LARGEST PARTY, ZULFIQAR ALI BHUTTO'S PAKISTAN PEOPLES PARTY (PPP), WINS ABOUT HALF THAT NUMBER: 81 OUT OF THE 138 SEATS IN WEST PAKISTAN.
RAHMAN EXPECTS TO BE INVITED TO FORM THE GOVERNMENT AT THE CENTRE. BUT AGHAST AT THE THOUGHT OF AN ASSEMBLY DOMINATED BY THE AWAMI LEAGUE, AND BULLIED BY BHUTTO WHO KEEPS HARPING ON MUJIB'S ALLEGED PRO-INDIA LEANINGS, YAHYA KHAN HEMS AND HAWS AND FINALLY POSTPONES THE UPCOMING SESSION OF THE PAKISTAN NATIONAL ASSEMBLY INDEFINITELY.

MEANWHILE, IN INDIA...
AFTER THE SUPREME COURT INVALIDATES THE ABOLITION OF PRIVY PURSES, MRS GANDHI DECIDES TO SEEK A FRESH MANDATE FROM THE PEOPLE.
CONGRESS को VOTE दीजिए
CONGRESS
AGAINST MRS GANDHI'S CONGRESS (R) IS RANGED A COALITION OF OPPOSITION PARTIES. THE OLD CONGRESS JOINS FORCES WITH THE SWATANTRA PARTY AND THE JANA SANGH. THE SLOGAN THEY CHOOSE IS 'INDIRA HATAAO!'
OVER EIGHT WEEKS, MRS GANDHI PLANS TO ATTEND 410 ELECTION MEETINGS AND ADDRESS AT LEAST 200 CRORE PEOPLE. BUT AS THE CARETAKER PRIME MINISTER OF THE COUNTRY, SHE CONTINUES TO KEEP UP WITH EVENTS IN PAKISTAN. HER PRINCIPAL SECRETARY P. N. HAKSAR BRIEFS HER REGULARLY.
YAHYA KHAN HAS REACHED DHAKA TODAY.
HMM. LET'S HOPE HIS DISCUSSIONS WITH MUJIB ARE PRODUCTIVE. AWAMI-LED PAKISTAN WILL NOT BE SO VICIOUSLY ANTI-INDIA.
THE FREQUENCY OF FLIGHTS FROM KARACHI TO DHAKA HAS GONE UP. LOTS OF YOUNG MEN IN PLAIN CLOTHES ARE ON THESE FLIGHTS. NOBODY KNOWS WHO THEY ARE.
SURELY, P. N., YOU ARE NOT SAYING THEY ARE MILITARY MEN IN MUFTI...?

R&AW IS PREPARING A REPORT FOR YOUR OFFICE. YOU'LL GET IT IN A FEW DAYS.
MADAM, THOUSANDS OF PEOPLE ARE WAITING AT THE NEXT VILLAGE CHOWK...
DON'T LAUGH, BABBOOJI!
OF ALL THE ODD THINGS I MUST DO...
THIS MIGHT BE...
THE VERY ODDEST!

WHAT IS BHUTTO SAYING?
HE IS TALKING ABOUT SHARING POWER. 'IDHAR HUM, UDHAR TUM' APPARENTLY.
THAT'S DISINGENUOUS. REMIND ME, PARMESHWAR, WHEN DID THE U.S. FORMALLY ANNOUNCE THE 'ONE TIME EXCEPTION' TO SUPPLYING MILITARY EQUIPMENT?
8 OCTOBER 1970. WASHINGTON GRANTED PAKISTAN NEARLY 50 MILLION DOLLARS' WORTH OF REPLACEMENT AIRCRAFT AND AROUND 300 PERSONNEL CARRIERS.
WOH KEHTE HAIN 'INDIRA HATAAO', MAIN KEHTI HOON 'GARIBI HATAAO'!
EARLY MARCH BRINGS GOOD NEWS. AT THE END OF WHAT IS INDIA'S MOST VIGOROUS GENERAL ELECTIONS SINCE 1947, CONGRESS (R) WINS 325 SEATS IN ALL.

RAJ NARAIN, CREATOR OF THE UNFORTUNATE 'INDIRA HATAAO' SLOGAN, WRESTLER-TURNED-SOCIALIST WHO CONTESTED AGAINST HER ON A CONGRESS (O) TICKET†, LOSES TO MRS GANDHI IN RAE BAREILLY BY OVER 1,10,000 VOTES.
THE ELECTIONS WERE RIGGED. I'LL GO TO COURT.
BARELY TWO DAYS DAY AFTER MRS GANDHI IS SWORN IN AS INDIA'S PRIME MINISTER FOR THE THIRD TIME, ON THE MORNING OF 19 MARCH, SHE RECEIVES A HIGHLY CLASSIFIED FILE AS SHE IS DOING YOGA. SHEIKH MUJIBUR RAHMAN HIMSELF HAS SENT HER A MESSAGE VIA THE INDIAN DEPUTY HIGH COMMISSIONER STATIONED IN DHAKA: 'EAST PAKISTAN HAS GONE TO THE POINT OF NO RETURN... NO ALTERNATIVE BUT TO FIGHT FOR INDEPENDENCE.'
CONFIDENT
INTELLIGENCE AGENCIES REPORT UNUSUAL ACTIVITIES AT THE BORDER.

THROUGHOUT MARCH, PROTESTERS THRONG THE STREETS OF DHAKA.
PADMA, MEGHANA, JAMUNA
TOMAAR AAMAAR THIKANA.
SHASHOK GOSHTHI KHATAM KAWRO! BANGLADESH SHAADHEEN KAWRO!
SHEIKH SHAHEB, WE NEED TO ESCAPE DHAKA IMMEDIATELY AND GO UNDERGROUND, THEN CROSS THE BORDER TO INDIA. ALL INDICATIONS SUGGEST AN ARMY CRACKDOWN.
TAJUDDIN, I CANNOT GO. THE ARMY WILL TORCH THE CITY LOOKING FOR ME. BUT I WANT YOU TO LEAVE RIGHT AWAY. BANGLADESH IS INDEPENDENT FROM THIS MOMENT; IT IS YOUR JOB TO CARRY THIS MESSAGE FAR AND WIDE.
SHEIKH MUJIB'S SACRIFICE IS IN VAIN. ON THE FATAL NIGHT OF 25 MARCH, TROOPS ROLL OUT OF THE CANTONMENT IN DHAKA AND POSITION THEMSELVES ACROSS THE CITY.
KILL THREE MILLION OF THEM... THE REST WILL EAT OUT OF OUR HANDS.

NEXT MORNING, SLEEPY SENTRIES AT THE VARIOUS INDIAN BORDER OUTPOSTS FIND A LONG LINE OF EMPTY-EYED PEOPLE SNAKING UP TO THE BORDER.
OVER THE NEXT FEW DAYS, AS DISSENTERS AND MEMBERS OF THE HINDU MINORITY ARE TARGETED IN EAST PAKISTAN, MRS GANDHI RECEIVES DETAILED REPORTS ON THE SITUATION.
THIS HOUSE EXPRESSES ITS DEEP ANGUISH AND GRAVE CONCERN AT THE RECENT DEVELOPMENTS IN EAST BENGAL. A MASSIVE ATTACK BY ARMED FORCES, DESPATCHED FROM WEST PAKISTAN, HAS BEEN UNLEASHED AGAINST THE ENTIRE PEOPLE OF EAST BENGAL WITH A VIEW TO SUPPRESSING THEIR URGES AND ASPIRATIONS.
WHILE SHE SPEAKS, TWO MEN SIT PENSIVELY ON A CULVERT NEAR THE INDO-PAK BORDER IN THE EAST. SINCE 25 MARCH, TAJUDDIN AHMAD, MUJIB'S DEPUTY AND SENIOR AWAMI LEAGUE LEADER, AND AMIRUL ISLAM HAVE TRAVELLED INCOGNITO, OFTEN WITHOUT FOOD OR WATER, ON FOOT AND ON HORSEBACK. THEIR GUIDE HAS GONE TO ESTABLISH CONTACT WITH THE INDIAN AUTHORITIES.

DO YOU THINK WE WILL BE ABLE TO MEET MRS GANDHI?
BEFORE WE EXPECT INDIA TO HELP US, WE NEED TO HAVE SOME KIND OF LEGITIMACY. MANY WILL ASK FOR A REVOLUTIONARY COUNCIL... ALONG THE LINES OF BIAFRA...
BEARING IN MIND THE PERMANENT INTERESTS WHICH INDIA HAS IN PEACE, AND COMMITTED AS WE ARE TO UPHOLD AND DEFEND HUMAN RIGHTS, THIS HOUSE DEMANDS IMMEDIATE CESSATION OF THE USE OF FORCE AND THE MASSACRE OF DEFENCELESS PEOPLE. THIS HOUSE CALLS UPON ALL PEOPLES AND GOVERNMENTS OF THE WORLD TO TAKE URGENT AND CONSTRUCTIVE STEPS TO PREVAIL UPON THE GOVERNMENT OF PAKISTAN TO PUT AN END IMMEDIATELY TO THE SYSTEMATIC DECIMATION OF PEOPLE WHICH AMOUNTS TO GENOCIDE.
BUT BIAFRA DID NOT SUCCEED! I FEEL WE SHOULD ESTABLISH A FORMAL GOVERNMENT OF BANGLADESH.
SHHH. DO YOU HEAR SOMETHING?
GOOD EVENING, SIR. WE HEARD A FEW SENIOR LEADERS MIGHT ARRIVE SEEKING POLITICAL ASYLUM... PERHAPS EVEN SHEIKH SHAHEB. ANY NEWS OF HIM?
SHEIKH SHAHEB REFUSED TO LEAVE DHAKA. YOU MUST CONSIDER ME HIS REPRESENTATIVE. ON BEHALF OF THE NEW NATION OF BANGLA DESH, WE WOULD LIKE TO MEET THE PRIME MINISTER OF INDIA. WOULD THAT BE POSSIBLE?

A HOT MID-APRIL DAY AT THE PRIME MINISTER'S RESIDENCE. MR R.N. KAO, THE HEAD OF R&AW, HAS COME FOR TEA. (EXCEPT, HE DOESN'T DRINK TEA.)
THE SWEARING-IN CEREMONY OF THE INTERIM GOVERNMENT OF BANGLADESH YESTERDAY, AT BAIDYANATH TALA, WENT WELL. INDIAN AND FOREIGN JOURNALISTS WERE PRESENT. UNFORTUNATELY, ONE OR TWO OF OUR BSF MEN IN UNIFORM WERE SPOTTED BY THE PRESS.
WE CAN'T AFFORD SUCH SLIP-UPS. THEY NEED TO BE MORE CAREFUL. PAKISTAN MIGHT HAVE LAUNCHED A GENOCIDE AGAINST ITS OWN CIVILIANS, RAMJI. BUT THE ENTIRE WORLD IS WATCHING US. ALL WEEK, I HAVE BEEN HEARING THINGS I DID NOT WANT TO HEAR. ONE MILLION REFUGEES IN INDIA AND COUNTING.
I HAVE GOVERNORS SITTING ON MY HEAD THE WHOLE DAY, COMPLAINING ABOUT THE REFUGE IN THEIR STATES. MY COUSIN, HIS EXCELLENC B.K., FOR ONE, FLEW DOWN TO COMPLAIN... NOW, SERIOUSLY, WHAT IS YOUR ASSESSMENT?

THERE IS NO SUGAR-COATING IT. THE SITUATION IS GOING TO GET MUCH WORSE. THE PAKISTANI ARMY WILL TARGET HINDUS. MORE REFUGEES WILL...
MY COLLEAGUES IN THE CABINET ARE TALKING ABOUT MILITARY OPTIONS. SAM WILL MAKE A PRESENTATION NEXT WEEK.
TILL NOW, WE HAVE BEEN QUITE RESTRAINED IN OUR SUPPORT TO BANGLA DESH. I KNOW EVERYONE IS TALKING OF WAR. BUT IN MY OPINION...
...AT THIS STAGE WAR WILL NOT BE OPTIMAL. WHAT WE NEED IS A PEOPLE'S WAR. GUERRILLA TACTICS. FOR THAT, WE HAVE TO CONSIDER ALL POSSIBILITIES.
UMM?
DID I MISS SOMETHING?
IS THE MUKTI FAUJ UP TO GUERRILLA TACTICS?
WE WILL NEED TO TRAIN THE VOLUNTEERS OURSELVES, PERHAPS RE-TRAIN A FEW OF THE FORCES.
WELL THEN, INDIA WILL DO WHAT INDIA MUST DO.

ON 25 APRIL, INDIRA GANDHI AND HER CABINET MINISTERS MEET THE COMMANDER-IN-CHIEF OF THE INDIAN ARMY, SAM MANECKSHAW.
PRIME MINISTER, I AM SORRY TO SAY, WAR IS NOT AN OPTION AT THE MOMENT. THE FORCES NEED TIME TO PREPARE. THE IMPENDING MONSOONS WILL PLAY HAVOC WITH MOBILITY AND OPERATIONS IN EAST PAKISTAN.
IF WE TAKE OVER OUR ROADS TO MOVE MILITARY EQUIPMENT TO THE BORDER, FOOD TRANSPORT WILL GET AFFECTED AND THERE MIGHT EVEN BE A FAMINE.
THE PASSES IN THE NORTH-EAST WILL REMAIN OPEN FOR THE NEXT FEW MONTHS, MAKING IT POSSIBLE FOR THE CHINESE TO INTERVENE...
EAST PAKISTAN
IN VIEW OF WHAT I SAID, PRIME MINISTER, IF YOU WISH FOR ME TO TENDER MY RESIGNATION...
THERE'S NO NEED TO GET DRAMATIC, SAM. BY WHEN DO YOU THINK YOUR FORCES WILL BE READY?
NOVEMBER.

OVER THE NEXT FEW WEEKS, THE REFUGEE CRISIS DEEPENS. BY 21 MAY, THERE ARE 3.5 MILLION REFUGEES IN INDIA, WITH 10,000 NEW REFUGEES POURING IN DAILY. MRS GANDHI SENDS EMISSARIES OUT TO TALK ABOUT THE HUMANITARIAN SITUATION. JAYPRAKASH NARAYAN IS ONE.
THE WORLD MUST KNOW WHAT PAKISTAN IS INFLICTING ON ITS OWN CITIZENS...
ON 7 JULY, MRS GANDHI MEETS HENRY KISSINGER, THE NATIONAL SECURITY ADVISER TO AMERICAN PRESIDENT RICHARD NIXON, IN NEW DELHI.
HOW LONG BEFORE THE PROBLEM TURNS UNMANAGEABLE?
IT IS UNMANAGEABLE RIGHT NOW. WE ARE JUST HOLDING IT TOGETHER BY SHEER WILLPOWER. AND WHILE YOUR ARMS SHIPMENT TO PAKISTAN MAY NOT MAKE A PRACTICAL DIFFERENCE TO INDIA, PSYCHOLOGICALLY THE U.S. HAS MADE THE SITUATION MUCH WORSE.
AS YOUNG BENGALI VOLUNTEERS ARE BEING TRAINED IN GUERRILLA WARFARE BY OFFICERS SUCH AS MAJOR-GENERAL SHABEG SINGH...
PAKISTAN IS LOOKING FOR NEW WAYS TO EMBARRASS THE GOVERNMENT OF INDIRA GANDHI. THEY INVITE THE LONDON-BASED DR JAGJIT SINGH CHAUHAN, SELF-APPOINTED SPOKESPERSON OF THE NASCENT 'KHALISTAN MOVEMENT', FOR A VISIT. ALTHOUGH HE HAS NO FOLLOWING IN PUNJAB, YAHYA KHAN LIONISES HIM AS A GREAT SIKH LEADER FROM INDIA.

MRS GANDHI ENDS HER EXTRAORDINARY DIPLOMATIC CAMPAIGN ABOUT INDIA'S POSITION ON THE EAST PAKISTAN CRISIS IN NOVEMBER, WITH A TRIP TO WASHINGTON.

INDIA ALSO COMMENDS YOUR ESTABLISHING RELATIONS FORMALLY WITH CHINA. DESPITE THE CHINESE ATTITUDE TO US, WE HAVE ALWAYS STOOD FOR PEACE AND STABILITY IN ASIA.
IS THE OLD WITCH GOING TO TALK ABOUT EAST PAKISTAN AT ALL?
I WISH TO UNDERLINE THAT INDIA CONTINUES TO REMAIN FIRMLY COMMITTED TO NON-ALIGNMENT IN FOREIGN POLICY.
THE LADY SURE KNOWS HOW TO PARLEY.
OH DEAR. THERE'S NO COMING BACK FROM THIS.
HAS BEEN VERY DIFFICULT FOR ME TO ET AWAY AT SUCH A CRITICAL TIME. BUT ANK YOU FOR HOSTING US.
AFTERWARDS...
I AM THE LEADER OF THE FREE WORLD!!! WHO THE HELL DOES SHE THINK SHE IS? THIS IS WHY I HATE INDIANS. YOU KNOW WHAT THE INDIANS NEED? THEY NEED A MASS FAMINE. POOR OLD YAHYA.
HOW'RE YOUR EYES? I BELIEVE YOU COULDN'T KEEP THEM OPEN AT DINNER LAST NIGHT?
DO YOU HAVE A BOOK I COULD BORROW FOR THE FLIGHT, PN? I NEED TO UNWIND.

3 DECEMBER 1971.
AAMI BANGLA BUJHTE PAARI, BOLTE PAARI NAA...
AIR
MRS GANDHI IS ADDRESSING A MASSIVE PUBLIC RALLY IN CALCUTTA ON 3 DECEMBER, AFTER HER RETURN FROM THE US, WHEN THE PAKISTAN AIR FORCE ATTACKS EIGHT OF INDIA'S FORWARD AIR-BASES.
TAPI TAPI
FORTUNATELY, R&AW HAS A MOLE IN YAHYA KHAN'S OFFICE, WHO HAS SENT PRIOR INTELLIGENCE ON THE ATTACKS. THE INDIAN AIRFORCE IS ON HIGH ALERT AND A DISASTER IS AVERTED. IAF PLANES ARE ABLE TO PURSUE THE PAF BOMBERS AND EVEN DAMAGE THE RUNWAYS IN EAST PAKISTAN.
AIR-INDIA
THANK GOD THEY ATTACKED FIRST. OTHERWISE WE'D HAVE HAD TO ATTACK BY NOW.

LANDING IN DELHI, SHE RUSHES TO THE MAP ROOM WHERE THE THREE CHIEFS WAIT TO BRIEF HER.
SUBSEQUENTLY, SHE MEETS THE CABINET AND THEN BRIEFS THE OPPOSITION LEADERS, INCLUDING ATAL BIHARI VAJPAYEE, WHO PLEDGE THEIR SUPPORT.
THE INDIAN FORCES ARE WELL PREPARED AND LED BY SOME OF THE FINEST MILITARY STRATEGISTS THE COUNTRY HAS PRODUCED. THANKS TO THE INTREPID FORCES OF THE MUKTI BAHINI, THEIR ON-GROUND INTELLIGENCE IS ALSO UNPARALLELED.

THE ALLIED FORCES (MITRO BAHINI) PROCEED SWIFTLY, AND ARE GREETED BY THE LOCAL POPULATION AS A LIBERATING ARMY.
ON 6 DECEMBER 1971, WITH THE FIRM CONVICTION THAT THE INDIAN ARMY WOULD REACH DHAKA SOON, MRS GANDHI RECOGNIZES THE NEW NATION OF BANGLADESH.
SHE HAS CROSSED ALL LIMITS. WE NEED TO DO SOMETHING FOR YAHYA...
THE INDIAN AMBASSADOR IN WASHINGTON, L.K. JHA, GETS A MYSTERIOUS PHONE CALL.
THE PRESIDENT HAS JUST GIVEN HIS ORDERS. THE NUCLEAR WARSHIP, USS ENTERPRISE, IS LEADING AN AMERICAN TASK FORCE TO THE BAY OF BENGAL.
L.K. JHA INFORMS DELHI IMMEDIATELY AND THE PRIME MINISTER DELIBERATES UPON OPTIONS.
PRIME MINISTER, MY TROOPS WILL BE IN DHAKA BEFORE NIXON'S NUKES ARRIVE...
ON 14 DECEMBER, INDIAN TANKS ADVANCE TOWARDS DHAKA BUT THIS TIME, WITH HAPPINESS WRIT ON THE FACE OF EVERY SOLDIER. THE WAR HAS CEASED AND PAKISTAN HAS AGREED TO SURRENDER.

LONG LIVE THE INDIAN ARMY!
THE PAKISTANI TROOPS WAIT LIKE TERRIFIED REFUGEES.
THERE'S NO NEED TO WORRY. THE INDIAN ARMY WILL ESCORT YOU TO THE SURRENDER AREAS. BUT DON'T GO OUT ON THE ROADS. THE MUKTI BAHINI MIGHT BE THERE.
GENERAL AURORA, ACCOMPANIED BY HIS CHIEF OF STAFF, MAJ. GEN. JFR JACOB, ARRIVES IN DHAKA.
IT HAD BEEN JACOB'S JOB TO CONVINCE GEN. NIAZI TO AGREE TO THE FINAL DRAFT OF THE INSTRUMENT OF SURRENDER.
A CALL IS PUT IN TO SOUTH BLOCK.

AT MRS GANDHI'S OFFICE IN PARLIAMENT, A SWEDISH TELEVISION TEAM IS FILMING AN INTERVIEW.
TRRRING!
YES...
YES...
THANK YOU.
PAKISTAN
YOU MUST EXCUSE ME, GENTLEMEN, FOR A COUPLE OF MINUTES. I HAVE AN ANNOUNCEMENT TO MAKE THAT THE HOUSE HAS BEEN WAITING FOR.

7

IN WHICH THERE IS AN EMERGENCY

There was no reply to Indira's email.

On Monday, school began. However, Miss Das did not come to class. A substitute teacher came instead, bossily took charge and completely pooh-poohed the oral history assignment on names. 'We need to focus on your CBSE syllabus. Okay?'

'Just as well,' whispered Happy to Indira. 'I had nothing to write on my name! No one remembers who named me. Mummy says it was Papa, Papa says it was Didi, Didi says it was Dadi. Uff. Mad lot, my family is.'

Tuesday.

Wednesday.

Thursday.

Friday.

There was no sign of Miss Das and no email from Piya didi.

It was a dull weekend. Happy came to the first Vanar Sena meeting, which had been scheduled for Sunday afternoon but found, much to his surprise, that Indira seemed rather dampened in her enthusiasm. He had to take on a leading role, which, of course, was nice in a way. But he felt somewhat cheated.

Next Monday, the substitute teacher told them that Miss Das's fellowship had ended. It had happened abruptly because the school and the NGO had, for some odd reason, broken up over the summer. Within a week, the divorce was full and final, and now school was back to regular programming and syllabi completion, with none of the naatak the teaching fellows did. All the students sighed and fidgeted for the rest of the day, groused about the new class-teacher who was not a patch on Miss Das's toe-nail, but Indira—Indira was devastated. She had planned her entire school career in her head with suitable interventions from Miss Das. 'She'll be back on WhatsApp soon, don't worry,' Happy tried to comfort her. 'We are friends with her outside of school, silly.' But that only wounded Indira further. If they were friends, wouldn't they have been informed before Miss Das and Piya didi disappeared from the face of the earth forever, along with that red-Nano-driving Rehaan.

The days crept past like drugged snails. Everything felt dull and colourless. Indira tried to immerse herself in the bland routine of her life again: school, tuition, homework, a few chores at home. Rinse. Repeat.

But there was a heavy feeling in her heart, a stone that seemed to get heavier and heavier by the day. She kept the little book on Indira Gandhi, which Piya didi had given her the first time and refused to take back, under her pillow; Arati framed the sketch Piya had made of her in Allahabad and hung it on the wall. However, neither the once-precious material objects, nor the memories did anything to dispel the miserable wet feeling in her soul, like a cloud that had become greyer and gloomier and floated about fatly but was unable to shower rain on the planet.

The third Saturday after school reopened, Happy and Indira walked up to the house and climbed the spiral staircase. There was a lock on the door; a bunch of bills and letters spilt out of the red letterbox. No one was home.

Thus it came to pass that on Sunday morning, 26 June, when Arati called Pal Singh in great agitation and requested him to drive Indira and herself to the Emergency Room in Safdarjung Hospital, it was Happy and his mother who arrived in Pal Singh's taxi. And Indira decided, once and for all, inside the Innova where she lay with her lips chapped and her throat dry while Navjot aunty dabbed her forehead with rosewater, as her eyes prickled and her throat felt lumpy and her lungs rasped for breath, that though it was not important, she needed to tell herself that she would never ever talk to Miss Das or Piya didi again.

ON 18 MAY 1974, DR K.P. MATHUR, THE MILD-MANNERED, POETRY-LOVING PHYSICIAN OF THE PRIME MINISTER, LEAVES 1 SAFDARJUNG ROAD SLIGHTLY BEWILDERED.
THIS MUST BE THE FIRST TIME SHE DIDN'T ASK ME TO SIT. WHAT'S GOING ON?
BRRRING!!
THE BUDDHA HAS SMILED.
WHAT?
TODAY IS BUDDHA JAYANTI. SOMEONE IS WISHING THE PM...
THEY ARE WRONG. IT IS A MESSAGE IN CODE. IN FARAWAY POKHRAN, SELECT PERSONNEL OF THE INDIAN MILITARY AND A FEW SCIENTISTS HAVE SUCCESSFULLY CONDUCTED INDIA'S FIRST PEACEFUL NUCLEAR TEST.

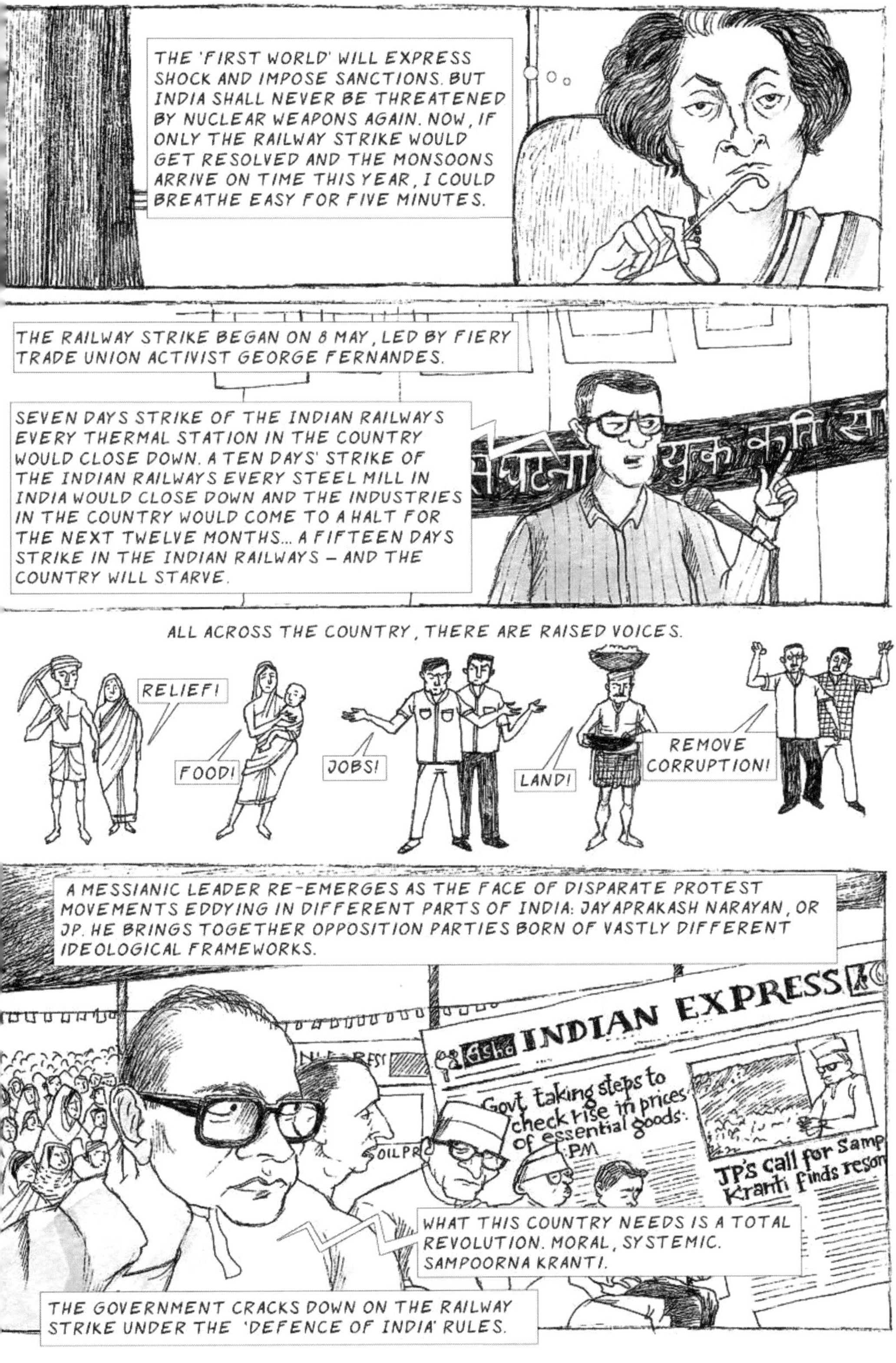
THE 'FIRST WORLD' WILL EXPRESS SHOCK AND IMPOSE SANCTIONS. BUT INDIA SHALL NEVER BE THREATENED BY NUCLEAR WEAPONS AGAIN. NOW, IF ONLY THE RAILWAY STRIKE WOULD GET RESOLVED AND THE MONSOONS ARRIVE ON TIME THIS YEAR, I COULD BREATHE EASY FOR FIVE MINUTES.
THE RAILWAY STRIKE BEGAN ON 8 MAY, LED BY FIERY TRADE UNION ACTIVIST GEORGE FERNANDES.
SEVEN DAYS STRIKE OF THE INDIAN RAILWAYS EVERY THERMAL STATION IN THE COUNTRY WOULD CLOSE DOWN. A TEN DAYS' STRIKE OF THE INDIAN RAILWAYS EVERY STEEL MILL IN INDIA WOULD CLOSE DOWN AND THE INDUSTRIES IN THE COUNTRY WOULD COME TO A HALT FOR THE NEXT TWELVE MONTHS... A FIFTEEN DAYS STRIKE IN THE INDIAN RAILWAYS – AND THE COUNTRY WILL STARVE.
ALL ACROSS THE COUNTRY, THERE ARE RAISED VOICES.
RELIEF!
FOOD!
JOBS!
LAND!
REMOVE CORRUPTION!
A MESSIANIC LEADER RE-EMERGES AS THE FACE OF DISPARATE PROTEST MOVEMENTS EDDYING IN DIFFERENT PARTS OF INDIA: JAYAPRAKASH NARAYAN, OR JP. HE BRINGS TOGETHER OPPOSITION PARTIES BORN OF VASTLY DIFFERENT IDEOLOGICAL FRAMEWORKS.
INDIAN EXPRESS
INDIAN
Govt taking steps to check rise in prices of essential goods: PM
WHAT THIS COUNTRY NEEDS IS A TOTAL REVOLUTION. MORAL, SYSTEMIC. SAMPOORNA KRANTI.
THE GOVERNMENT CRACKS DOWN ON THE RAILWAY STRIKE UNDER THE 'DEFENCE OF INDIA' RULES.

AS THE POLITICAL CLIMATE HOTS UP, FOUR FRIENDS CATCH UP IN THE INDIAN COFFEE HOUSE AT JANPATH, NEW DELHI.
DID YOU SEE THE NUMBER OF PEOPLE AT JP'S RALLY? FROM AHMEDABAD TO PATNA, FROM THE WEST TO THE EAST, THE YOUNG ARE COMING TOGETHER AGAINST INDIRA GANDHI'S NEPOTISM.
IT'S A REVOLUTION ALL RIGHT. THE CONGRESS WILL BE SWEPT AWAY.
WHY DON'T THEY WAIT FOR THE ELECTIONS? INDIRA GANDHI IS A DEMOCRATICALLY ELECTED LEADER AFTER ALL.
TELL ME WHAT DEMOCRATICALLY ELECTED POSITION SANJAY HOLDS? DO YOU KNOW HOW POWERFUL HE AND HIS CRONIES HAVE BECOME?
I DON'T BELIEVE IN ALL THESE GHERAOS AND STRIKES.

BY THE END OF 1974, SANJAY GANDHI, THE PRIME MINISTER'S YOUNGER SON, HAS RISEN TO BE HER MOST TRUSTED LIEUTENANT. WHILE HE SPENDS MOST OF HIS TIME TRYING TO BUILD AN INDIGENOUS PEOPLE'S CAR, THE MARUTI, HE ALSO ADVISES MRS GANDHI ON MANY MATTERS.
IN NOVEMBER 1974, A MEETING IS FINALLY ARRANGED BETWEEN MRS GANDHI AND JP.
FOR A MOMENT, WHEN THEY MEET, THEY REMEMBER OLD TIMES.
YOU DON'T SEEM TO REALIZE THAT YOUR ACTIONS ARE INIMICAL TO DEMOCRACY.
IT IS TIME TO SAVE DEMOCRACY...
DO YOU EVEN KNOW THAT HALF THE ELEMENTS IN YOUR SO-CALLED REVOLUTION ARE IN THE EMPLOY OF THE CIA?
INDU! THESE CANNOT BE YOUR THOUGHTS, YOUR WORDS. I NEVER THOUGHT PANDITJI'S DAUGHTER WOULD BECOME A... SOVIET STOOGE!
HOT WORDS ARE EXCHANGED AND NO COMMON GROUND IS FOUND.

BUT AFTERWARDS, JP WISHES TO SPEAK TO MRS GANDHI IN PRIVATE.
INDU, THESE ARE KAMALA'S LETTERS TO PRABHA. I FOUND THEM WHEN I WAS GOING THROUGH HER THINGS, AFTER HER DEMISE.
THANK YOU.
CONVEY MY BLESSINGS TO RAJIV'S CHILDREN AND TO SANJAY'S YOUNG BRIDE.
DO TAKE CARE OF YOUR HEALTH.
ON 12 JUNE 1975, THE ALLAHABAD HIGH COURT UNSEATS MRS GANDHI ON 'ELECTORAL MALPRACTICES'. ALL HELL BREAKS LOOSE.

COFFEE HOUSE. RAVI, MALA, GURMEET AND NAFISA CATCH UP.
IT'S A CRYING SHAME! UNSEATING A PRIME MINISTER OVER NOTHING.
WHAT NOTHING? HER PRIVATE SECRETARY'S RESIGNATION WAS NOT ACCEPTED TILL 25 JANUARY. BUT HE STARTED WORKING AS HER ELECTION AGENT FROM THE 13TH. IT'S AGAINST THE RULES OF THE ELECTION COMMISSION.
DRACONIAN RULES!
IT'S THE BEGINNING OF THE END FOR INDIRA GANDHI.
AND WHAT OF THE COUNTRY? JP AND COMPANY ARE SHOUTING FROM THE ROOFTOPS, ASKING FOR HER RESIGNATION. BUT WHAT WILL HAPPEN AFTERWARDS? WHO WILL MANAGE THE ECONOMY?
HOPEFULLY SOMEONE WHO WILL STEER IT TOWARDS REFORM. MORARJI BHAI WOULD MAKE A GREAT PRIME MINISTER.
HOLD YOUR HORSES. I AM SURE THE SUPREME COURT WILL ORDER AN UNCONDITIONAL STAY.

MEANWHILE, THE OPPOSITION HAS TAKEN THE BATTLE TO THE STREETS.
RATH KA GHAR GHAR NAAD SUNO SINGHAASAN KHAALI KARO KI JANTAA AATI HAI...
JP TELLS GOVERNMENT SERVANTS, BUREAUCRATS, POLICE AND ARMY OFFICERS THAT SINCE THE GOVERNMENT HAS LOST ITS MORAL AUTHORITY TO LEAD, THEY ARE NO LONGER DUTY-BOUND TO FOLLOW 'ILLEGAL AND UNCONSTITUTIONAL ORDERS'.
REACTING TO THIS, INDIRA GANDHI DECIDES TO DECLARE A NATIONAL EMERGENCY IN RESPONSE TO 'INTERNAL DISTURBANCES' THAT VERY NIGHT.
THERE DOESN'T SEEM TO BE ANY OTHER WAY...
THE TIME IS RIGHT.
THE PRESIDENT'S SIGNATURE IS OBTAINED ON THE PROCLAMATION. POLICE OFFICERS ACROSS THE COUNTRY ARE ORDERED TO GO OUT INTO THE NIGHT AND ARREST MEMBERS OF THE OPPOSITION AS WELL AS OTHER LEADERS. MORARJI DESAI AND JP ARE TAKEN TO A GUEST HOUSE IN HARYANA.

VARIOUS POLITICAL ACTIVISTS FIND THEMSELVES BEHIND BARS, DETAINED UNDER MISA OR DIR.
NEWSPAPER OFFICES IN THE CAPITAL FIND THEMSELVES WITHOUT ELECTRICITY. CENSORSHIP HAS BEEN IMPOSED.
THE OPPOSITION PARTIES HAD CHALKED OUT A PROGRAMME OF COUNTRYWIDE GHERAOS. ONE OF THEM WENT TO THE EXTENT OF SAYING THAT ARMED FORCES SHOULD NOT CARRY OUT ORDERS... THIS WOULD HAVE RESULTED IN A GRAVE THREAT TO PUBLIC ORDER AND DAMAGE TO THE ECONOMY BEYOND REPAIR...
POLICE
POLICE
NDIAN HERALD
SPECIAL SUPPLEMENT
EMERGENCY DECLARED
JP, MORARJI, ADVANI, ASOKA MEHTA & VAJPAYEE ARRESTED
A DEATHLY SILENCE FALLS ON THE COUNTRY. THE OPPOSITION BENCHES ARE EMPTY IN PARLIAMENT. THE PRESS COUNCIL IS ABOLISHED; 26 ANTI-CONGRESS POLITICAL ORGANIZATIONS ARE BANNED, INCLUDING THE RSS AND THE CPI(M) AND CPI(M-L).

IN THE NEXT FEW MONTHS, SANJAY GANDHI AND HIS COTERIE CONSOLIDATE POWER, RUNNING A PARALLEL SECRATARIAT TO THE PRIME MINISTER'S OFFICE.
AS MRS GANDHI FOCUSSES ON ECONOMICS, SMUGGLERS AND BLACK MARKETERS ARE APPREHENDED, PRICES FALL, TRAINS RUN ON TIME AND GOVERNMENT BABUS DON'T SIT ON FILES. ON THE SURFACE IT SEEMS AS THOUGH A NEW ERA OF ORDER AND DISCIPLINE HAS DAWNED. HOWEVER, WITH ITS HARD-WON FREEDOM FETTERED, THE SOUL OF INDIA IS DYING.
S C SHARMA & CO
snowhite
ALLWYN WATCHES
I HAVE LABELLED ALL MY GOODS, BABA!
HEY! WHO ORDERED THIS DEMOLITION?
HEHE! WHAT DEMOLITION? 'THIS IS 'BEAUTIFICATION'.

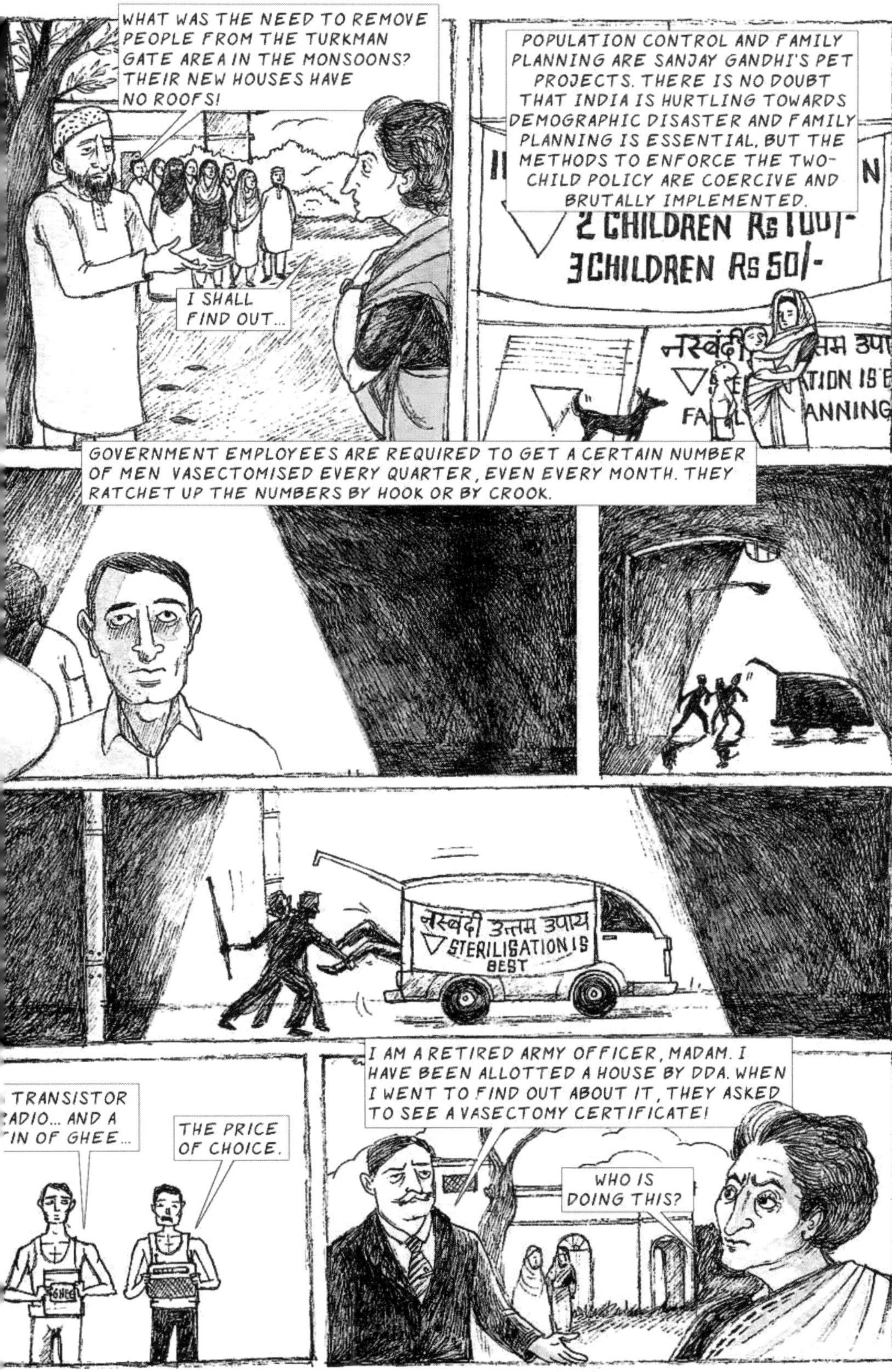
WHAT WAS THE NEED TO REMOVE PEOPLE FROM THE TURKMAN GATE AREA IN THE MONSOONS? THEIR NEW HOUSES HAVE NO ROOFS!
I SHALL FIND OUT...
POPULATION CONTROL AND FAMILY PLANNING ARE SANJAY GANDHI'S PET PROJECTS. THERE IS NO DOUBT THAT INDIA IS HURTLING TOWARDS DEMOGRAPHIC DISASTER AND FAMILY PLANNING IS ESSENTIAL, BUT THE METHODS TO ENFORCE THE TWO-CHILD POLICY ARE COERCIVE AND BRUTALLY IMPLEMENTED.
2 CHILDREN Rs 100/-
3CHILDREN Rs 50/-
GOVERNMENT EMPLOYEES ARE REQUIRED TO GET A CERTAIN NUMBER OF MEN VASECTOMISED EVERY QUARTER, EVEN EVERY MONTH. THEY RATCHET UP THE NUMBERS BY HOOK OR BY CROOK.
नस्बंदी उत्तम उपाय
STERILISATION IS BEST
TRANSISTOR ADIO... AND A IN OF GHEE...
GHEE
THE PRICE OF CHOICE.
I AM A RETIRED ARMY OFFICER, MADAM. I HAVE BEEN ALLOTTED A HOUSE BY DDA. WHEN I WENT TO FIND OUT ABOUT IT, THEY ASKED TO SEE A VASECTOMY CERTIFICATE!
WHO IS DOING THIS?

MONTHS ROLL BY...
INDIAN COFFEE HOUSE, JANPATH.
RAVI! LONG TIME!
IT'S NOT SAFE FOR YOU TO TALK TO THE LIKES OF ME.
WHERE IS MALA?

SHE'S IN TIHAR JAIL. SHE WAS IMPRISONED ALMOST A YEAR AGO.
I'M SORRY TO HEAR THAT.
WELL, I'LL BE HONEST, MY FATHER FORCED ME TO SIGN A PETITION SUPPORTING MRS GANDHI'S 20-POINT PROGRAMME. I DIDN'T WANT TO END UP IN PRISON TOO. MALA'S MORE IDEALISTIC. I GO SEE HER SOMETIMES.
I KNOW YOU DON'T AGREE WITH MY VIEWS, RAVI, BUT ON THE WHOLE, ISN'T IT QUIETER, NICER? PRICES HAVE COME DOWN. MAYBE IN A POOR COUNTRY LIKE OURS, DEMOCRACY WAS ALWAYS A LUXURY.
DON'T SAY THAT!
WHAT CAN I SAY? EVEN OUR LEADER DEORASJI HAS WRITTEN LETTERS TO MRS GANDHI FROM PRISON, PRAISING HER 20-POINT PROGRAMME. THE OPPOSITION IS BROKEN. GAYATRI DEVI, BIJU PATNAIK, THEY'VE ALL SOFTENED THEIR STANCES. JP, I HEAR, IS SUFFERING FROM SERIOUS HEALTH ISSUES EVER SINCE HIS RELEASE.
THE EMERGENCY WILL NEVER END...
AND YET, AS EVERYONE SEEMS TO BE ADJUSTING TO A NEW NORMAL, MRS GANDHI GOES AGAINST SANJAY AND OTHER ADVISERS . . .

18 JANUARY 1977. ON A COLD, RAINY DAY AT THE KUMBHA MELA IN SANGAM, MRS GANDHI'S HELICOPTER IS SIGHTED.
ELECTIONS HAVE BEEN SCHEDULED FOR MARCH. OPPOSITION LEADERS WILL BE RELEASED IMMEDIATELY. PRESS CENSORSHIP IS TO BE LIFTED...
I NEVER THOUGHT THIS DAY WOULD COME.

THE END COMES AS SWIFTLY AS THE BEGINNING. IN RAM LILA MAIDAN, THE OPPOSITION ORGANIZES ITS BIG RALLY. HUNDREDS OF THOUSANDS OF RICKSHAW-WALLAHS, SMALL TRADERS, GRANDMOTHERS AND STUDENTS HUDDLE TOGETHER.
SEE HOW MANY PEOPLE HAVE COME EVEN THOUGH DOORDARSHAN IS SHOWING 'BOBBY'...
SHH! ATALJI IS GOING TO SPEAK.

BAAD MUDDAT KE MILE HAIN DEEWANE,
KEHNE SUNNE KO BAHUT HAIN AFSANE,
KHULI HAWA MEIN ZARAA SAANS TOH LE LEIN
KAB TAK RAHEGI AAZAADI KAUN JAANE?

A FEW KILOMETRES AWAY, AT 1 SAFDARJUNG ROAD, MRS GANDHI FEELS A SUDDEN SHARP STAB IN HER HEART.
WILL WE LOSE?

8

IN WHICH WE MEET DIDA

Twice or thrice a year, a regular day in a regular week, Piya would suddenly find it impossible to get out of bed in the morning. She would remain under the sheets, as though flattened to the mattress by a gigantic beam that had separated at night from the cosmos and picked her out from among the seven billion people on the planet.

As the sun marked the sky, a blue ball sitting in the middle of her forehead would pulsate. Thin lines of pain would radiate from it, shooting up and down and flipping sideways into far corners of her brain. She would not feel hungry or thirsty—and most disconcertingly for everyone around her, even when she dragged herself up from the bed, she would find herself unable to lift a pencil or a brush and hold it to paper. Sometimes she would feel such a burst of panic about her state that she would go back and bury herself deep under the sheets, hoping to hide there forever. Sometimes she would have no energy at all to panic or get worked up, and tears would leak out of her eyes continuously, and the pillows would get wet.

They had returned from Allahabad two nights ago. The next day, Reema unpacked and cleaned cheerfully, bustled over her syllabus plan and cooked for Rehaan and his colleagues, while Piya went over her notes and transferred photographs from her camera to her laptop and chatted with the comedy boys who were all, to different degrees, in love with her.

When Reema returned early next morning from the all-night comedy competition, well in time for school, she found Piya flattened to the bed, tear-tracks streaking her face. An hour later, her advisor at the NGO called and Reema found out that, no thanks to a bunch of technicalities no one had taken into account, she was out of a job.

She called the most sensible person she knew: Piya's mother.

Dr Chatterjee was a scientist in Bangalore. While Piya's dad would have fallen apart at the renewed cycle of her depression, Piya's mother knew exactly what would work. Reema would often joke that *she* was the real daughter to Dr Chatterjee. The two were exactly alike: practical, solution-oriented, non-dramatic. The first thing that Dr Chatterjee did after Reema's sober phone call was wire three months' rent to their landlady. Then she spoke to her mother, Piya's beloved Dida, and told her that Piya would reach sooner than expected.

'Why don't you and Rehaan also go and stay with Dida for a few days, Reema?' Dr Chatterjee asked.

'Take a break from Delhi? Actually, that's not such a bad idea, Aunty,' Reema replied. 'We've wanted to go trekking for a while.'

The next day, Reema packed Piya's books on Indira Gandhi, her art work, colours, brushes and pencils with meticulous care, jammed them into the red Nano, and the three of them set off for the hills. Unlike the trip to Allahabad, which was full of chatter and bravado, this was a silent journey. And by the time they reached Dida's cottage, fifty kilometres above Vashishth in Manali, even their phones had fallen silent. There was no network. Only birdsong and the brown noise of their brains.

The first week, Piya remained confined to Dida's bedroom for most of the day. Dida did not ask any questions—knowing there was no logic whatsoever to the dislodged beam that had trapped Piya's heart. She just brought her soup three times a day—the only thing Piya could bring herself to eat. She brushed her hair and drew her hot baths and played old Hindi songs on the radio when she sensed she could.

The second week, Piya went down to the garden with Dida, and sat in silence as Dida talked while shelling pods and knitting sweaters and giving advice to the gardener and sticking photographs in old albums.

In the third week, Piya asked for mutton curry and rice on Sunday and spoke to her parents on the phone, once.

As the fourth week commenced, she opened the boxes that Reema had so lovingly packed and laid out the brushes and paints on her desk. Dida and her gang of staff-members breathed a collective sigh of relief. 'Piya baby has her paints out,' they told each other. 'Let's send one of the cute kids from the village to her room right away. Or one of the new kittens in a basket. She will start painting immediately.'

By the fifth week, Piya began to feel like herself again. She missed Reema, missed Indira, even missed Happy. She began to tell Dida about the kids, their Vanar Sena, her book. But she couldn't bring herself to speak on the phone. She helped Maniya's grandchildren with their homework in the evenings, but she couldn't bear to check her email.

Some mornings, after Piya had worked all night, she would join Dida for breakfast. Round the year, Dida woke up at 4:45 a.m., did yoga, bathed, worshipped her deities, then sat down for a cup of Darjeeling tea with toast at six, just as the sky began to blue. Piya would be stretching her arms and legs on the living-room carpet after a productive night (she had started working on a large canvas again and her arms ached in the morning), when Dida would come downstairs. 'Again you haven't slept all night?' she would ask, raising her eyebrows in mock severity. 'What are we going to do with you?'

Dida, her old pink shawl wrapped around her, smelling of lavender and oranges, would throw open the heavy door and walk out to the garden, sniffing the sweet-smelling air outside. Afterwards, she would sit in the porch, where breakfast would be brought on a large tray by Maniya along with a digest of local gossip. Certain rituals had remained constant over the two decades of Piya's remembered life: Maniya; the teapot swaddled in an old woollen tea cosy; toast neatly stacked; the day's newspaper; homemade jam and marmalade; and her favourite, Dida's chunky peanut butter.

On these mornings, after Dida descended, Piya would trail her like she used to as a child, and sit noiselessly at the edge of a chair, suddenly unsure of her limbs. She would be sleepy but also weirdly energetic; she would be flooded with nostalgia for the past when she spent summer after summer in this delightful house, but simultaneously there would be this strange mix of anxiety about the future. One part of her would race forward, completely unattached again, from this childhood nest where she came to escape all the noise and madness of the Delhi attic, with its constant stream of visitors, or her parents' house in Bangalore, where she invariably regressed into being a sulky teenager.

'What were you working on last night?' Dida asked this morning, pouring her a cup of tea and lovingly slathering peanut butter on toast for her.

'Nothing in particular,' Piya mumbled.

'What happened to the show that was going to be held in September?'

'I pulled out, Dida,' Piya replied. 'I'm not going to be able to do any major work in time.'

'What happened to that boy who came to visit you last summer? The Malayali?'

'Oh, he's busy… travelling… I don't have time. My book has to be finished.'

'I don't see you working on the book. You're making canvases.'

'I know, I know,' Piya said, sounding tormented again.

'I asked only because I want to read the book,' Dida said, carefully. 'You know how much I love Indira Gandhi. That's why I named you Priyadarshini.' Dida chuckled. 'Your parents weren't so happy with that. And your Mala mausi refused to speak to me for months.'

Piya knew the story backwards. But she liked hearing it.

'So how exactly are we related to Mala mausi?' she asked, though she knew the answer well enough. Mala mausi's mother and Dida were first cousins.

Mala mausi was a firebrand student activist, secretary of the Delhi University students' union; she had spent many months in prison during the Emergency. She was a sort of mentor to Piya's parents. Piya's mother was still quite young in the early seventies, in school. But when the JP movement was gathering steam in Bihar, Piya's dad had just entered college. He was swept away by JP's charisma and joined his movement. In 1975, after JP gave the call for 'Total Revolution' or 'Sampoorna Kranti', Papa came to Delhi on a whim, along with a bunch of college seniors. They had neither money, nor a place to stay. Through the political grapevine, they met Mala mausi. She divided them up and distributed them across various homes in the city. Papa was allotted to Dadu and Dida's house (Dadu was a statistician at the Indian Statistical Institute) and that was how, right under Dida's nose, Mama and Papa fell in love.

'So, Dida, how did Papa manage to fool you?'

'He didn't fool me one bit,' Dida said, 'I always knew he was a JP Socialist. Still is, at heart. Idealistic fool. Used to go to those rallies at Ram Lila maidan, return with eyes shining. But since he was from out of town, there was no warrant issued for him when the Emergency was declared. He stayed on in Delhi for a while longer, anticipating a warrant back home in Bihar. But I didn't mind. It wasn't like it is nowadays. People screaming bloody murder at those who disagree with their politics. Your father was a nice handsome boy, concerned about the country. And JP was a hero of the freedom struggle, don't forget.'

Piya yawned.

'Dida,' she said, 'I think I'll go and sleep now. Reema and Rehaan might come today.'

'All right,' said Dida. 'I'll make lunch for the lot of you. Go up and rest for a while now. I have a lot of work to do.'

'It was incredible,' Reema gushed. 'Blue skies. Clean air. Radio silence. I know we meant to stay for only a fortnight. But the hotel gave us a better rate for a month, and Rehaan came up with two new acts for his standup group. I slept and read and wondered what to do with my life. It was wonderful, Piya. Why do we live such pointlessly busy lives in Delhi, again?'

Piya laughed and nibbled at the yak cheese they had brought.

'I've got so many second-hand books for Indira's library,' Reema told them. 'There was a wonderful second-hand bookshop there. Anyway, once I am back, since I am jobless, maybe I'll join her Vanar Sena! Try to make a career out of that.'

'Oh, so she was serious?' Rehaan asked.

'Of course,' said Reema. 'She's dead serious about everything. The Vanar Sena will start a library for children in Basant Gaon, I told you.'

'And I've been asked to design the logo and a poster, and I *might* have to give free paintings to big donors,' Piya replied. 'When did you last speak to her, Reema?'

Miss Das flushed. She'd kept thinking she would call Arati, but somehow Spiti Valley had consumed her.

'Didn't you check your email?' she replied defensively, 'Indira had said she would write to you.'

IN THE ELECTIONS OF 1977, MRS GANDHI AND SANJAY BOTH LOSE THEIR SEATS.
THE CONGRESS IS DECIMATED IN THE NORTH.
AFTER LOSING THE ELECTIONS, FOR A WHILE MRS GANDHI FINDS HERSE UNMOORED. SHE'S 59, WITH HARDLY ANY MONEY OR A PERMANENT ADDRESS.
PRIME MINISTER MORARJI DESAI DECIDES TO MOVE INTO 1 SAFDARJUNG ROAD EVEN THOUGH HIS EXISTING HOUSE IS LARGER.
EVENTUALLY, MOHD YUNUS MAKES 12 WILLINGDON CRESCENT AVAILABLE TO THE GANDHIS.
MRS GANDHI AND HER FAMILY MOVE THERE. BY NOW, THE SERVANTS AND SECRETARIES HAVE MELTED AWAY.
SOON, SHE FINDS HERSELF THE TARGET OF A JANATA PARTY-LED WITCH HUNT.
IN EARLY JULY 1977, IN BELCHI, A REMOTE VILLAGE IN BIHAR, DALITS ARE MASSACRED BY UPPER-CASTE LANDOWNERS.
MRS GANDHI RUSHES TO BIHAR.
I DON'T THINK WE SHOULD VENTURE AHEAD, MADAM.
DESPITE WARNINGS AT BIHARSHARIF, SHE PLOUGHS AHEAD THROUGH THE RAIN AND MUD. SOON HER JEEP HAS TO BE TOWED BY A TRACTOR.

SHE HITCHES A RIDE ON MOTI. IN BELCHI, THE VILLAGERS RUSH TO HER WITH THEIR HAIR-RAISING TALES. MRS GANDHI OFFERS THEM THE ONLY THING SHE CAN – HER CONCERN.
ON THE WAY BACK, HER BOAT SINKS MID-RIVER, AND SHE WADES TO THE MAINLAND IN THE DARK. THERE THE LOCAL WOMEN HAVE GATHERED...
E DIDN'T VOTE FOR OU THE LAST TIME.
PLEASE HAVE SOME PURI-HALWA. YOU HAVEN'T EATEN ALL DAY.
THANK YOU FOR COMING.

BY MID-1979, FACTIONALISM AND INTERNAL RIVALRY HAVE WEAKENED THE JANATA GOVERNMENT CONSIDERABLY. ELECTIONS ARE HELD IN JANUARY 1980, AND AIDED BY A CHASTENED SANJAY, MRS GANDHI MAKES A THRILLING POLITICAL COMEBACK. CONGRESS(I) WINS 351 SEATS.

14 JANUARY 1980, SHE'S SWORN IN AS PRIME MINISTER FOR THE FOURTH TIME AND, SOON AFTER, SHE MEETS HER OLD FRIEND, R.N. KAO.
SO WHAT GOOD NEWS HAVE YOU COMPILED FOR ME, RAMJI?
THE CIA AND ISI ARE TRAINING 'MUJAHIDEENS' TO COUNTER THE SOVIETS IN AFGHANISTAN. IT'S PLAYING WITH FIRE. IF YOU ASK ME, WE NEED TO MONITOR KASHMIR CLOSELY.
HMM...
THE AKALIS ARE NOT HELPING MATTERS EITHER. REMEMBER DR JAGJIT SINGH CHAUHAN, WHOM YAHYA LIONISED IN '71? HE HAD QUIETENED DOWN IN THE JANATA YEARS AND RETURNED TO INDIA. BUT AS WE SPEAK, HE'S BACK IN LONDON AND HAS RESTARTED THE KHALISTAN MOVEMENT.
PLEASE DON'T TELL ME THERE'S MORE!
EVER SINCE MUJIB'S ASSASSINATION, BANGLADESH HAS ONCE AGAIN BECOME A HUB OF ANTI-INDIA ACTIVITIES DIRECTED TOWARDS OUR NORTH-EAST. THERE MIGHT BE BAD NEWS FROM ASSAM OR TRIPURA.

BUT NO ONE COULD HAVE IMAGINED WHAT WAS TO COME NEXT.
ON 23 JUNE 1980, THREE MONTHS AFTER THE BIRTH OF HIS SON, SANJAY GANDHI DIES IN A PLANE CRASH AT SAFDARJUNG AIRFIELD. HE WAS ONLY 33.

MONTHS GO BY. IN MAY 1981, NEARLY A YEAR AFTER SANJAY'S DEATH, RAJIV GANDHI ANNOUNCES HE WILL CONTEST BY-ELECTIONS FROM AMETHI, SANJAY'S CONSTITUENCY.
MANEKA, WHO FEELS SHE IS THE TRUE INHERITOR OF SANJAY'S LEGACY, IS DEEPLY UNHAPPY.
RAJIV'S FIRST ASSIGNMENT IS TO PREPARE NEW DELHI FOR THE ASIAN GAMES WHICH ARE HELD UNDER THE AEGIS OF THE OLYMPIC COUNCIL OF ASIA. THE ASIAD IS A HUGE SUCCESS.

4 DECEMBER 1982.
CLOSING CEREMONY DAY.
AT 1 SAFDARJUNG ROAD, THERE IS TREMENDOUS HUSTLE AND BUSTLE. AMITABH AND AJITABH BACHCHAN, ARUN SINGH AND ARUN NEHRU, RAJIV GANDHI'S CLOSEST FRIENDS, HAVE ALL GATHERED THERE WITH THEIR FAMILIES, AND IN THE EVENING, A LARGE PARTY LEAVES FOR THE VENUE. ACCIDENTALLY, P, MRS GANDHI'S 10-YEAR-OLD GRAND-DAUGHTER, GETS LEFT BEHIND IN CLASSIC HOME ALONE FASHION. SHE GULPS DOWN HER TEARS, PUTS ON A BRAVE FACE AND REPORTS TO DADI THAT SHE MIGHT HAVE ENJOYED THE FIREWORKS, BUT THEN AGAIN, SHE MIGHT JUST READ A BOOK.
MRS GANDHI STEPS OUT AND FINDS A VAN. TOGETHER THE TWO OF THEM FIND A VANTAGE POINT FROM WHERE THE FIREWORKS OF SIRI FORT ARE VISIBLE. P PONDERS UPON THE LIGHTS AND COLOURS, MRS GANDHI MARKS FILES INSIDE. FOR A FLEETING SECOND, SHE REMEMBERS HOW SANJAY HAD A PHASE WHEN HE WOULD TRY TO MAKE HIS OWN FIREWORKS.

IN 1983, A YOUNG SCIENTIST, A.P.J. ABDUL KALAM, THEN THE HEAD OF DEFENCE RESEARCH AND DEVELOPMENT LABORATORY (DRDL), SEEKS A MEETING WITH THE PRIME MINISTER.
MADAM, WE NEED SELF-SUFFICIENCY IN MISSILE TECHNOLOGY. WE CANNOT DEPEND ON THE LARGESSE OF FOREIGN COUNTRIES...
IT WILL REQUIRE A SIGNIFICANT OUTLAY.
HOW MUCH?
350 CRORES.
350 CRORES? THAT'S A LOT OF MONEY. THERE ARE SO MANY TROUBLES ON ALL FRONTS, DR KALAM.
BUT WITHOUT INDIGENISATION, WE SHALL ALWAYS HAVE MORE TROUBLE.
WELL THEN. HOW ABOUT I MEET YOUR BRIGHTEST SCIENTISTS UNDER THE AGE OF 35? I NEED TO SEE WHO WILL BE THERE AFTER I AM GONE, AND IF THE YOUNG PEOPLE ARE TRULY COMMITTED TO INDIGENISATION.
WE CAN DO THAT.
IN JULY 1983, BEFORE THE KHALISTAN CRISIS TAKES OVER THE NATIONAL NARRATIVE, MRS GANDHI MEETS THE YOUNG SCIENTISTS IN SOUTH BLOCK.
VK saraswat
THERE YOU GO. I HAVE SANCTIONED THE ENTIRE AMOUNT. I SHALL NOT BE THERE TO OVERSEE IT. I TRUST YOU WILL COMPLETE IT.

1983
1982
1983
THOUGH THE SITUATION IS TENSE IN ASSAM AND PUNJAB, AND THE TAMIL– SINHALA WAR IN SRI LANKA HAS REACHED A FLASHPOINT, NEW DELHI HOSTS THE MEMORABLE NON-ALIGNED MOVEMENT SUMMIT IN MID 1983.
LIKE NEHRU, MRS GANDHI, BY THEN, IS ONE OF THE WORLD'S MOST RECOGNISABLE LEADERS.
THE SUMMER OF 1983. INDIA AND WEST INDIES ARE PLAYING A HISTORIC MATCH...
HEY FAROKH, DO YOU THINK MRS GANDHI IS LISTENING...?
DO YOU THINK SHE WILL DECLARE A PUBLIC HOLIDAY IF INDIA WINS?
YOU DON'T KNOW HOW MUCH SHE LOVES CRICKET, BRIAN.
ABSOLUTELY!
WITHIN 5 MINUTES A PHONE CALL FROM THE INDIAN CABINET IS RELAYED... MRS GANDHI HAS HEARD THEM...

BY LATE 1983, THE KHALISTAN PROBLEM HAS BLOWN UP TO TERRIBLE PROPORTIONS.

ON THE NIGHT OF 5 JUNE, THE INDIAN ARMY STORMS INTO THE HARMANDIR SAHIB, UNDER THE LEADERSHIP OF LT. GEN. K.S. BRAR. DUE TO POOR INTELLIGENCE ABOUT THE LEVEL OF PREPAREDNESS OF BHINDRANWALE'S MEN (THEY KNEW THE COMPLEX INSIDE OUT, THEY HAD HUGE QUANTITIES OF AMMUNITION AND ARMS SOURCED FROM PAKISTAN AND CHINA, AND THEY EVEN HAD ROCKET LAUNCHERS), THE ARMY SUFFERS GREAT LOSSES. BY THE MORNING OF 7 JUNE, THE TEMPLE IS IN THEIR CONTROL. HOWEVER, THE AKAL TAKHT HAS BEEN BADLY DAMAGED OWING TO THE DEPLOYMENT OF TANKS. JARNAIL SINGH BHINDRANWALE HAS BEEN KILLED.

NO ONE WOULD HAVE THOUGHT THE HARMANDIR SAHIB WOULD SEE SUCH A GUN BATTLE.
I AM NO FAN OF MRS GANDHI. BUT WHAT OPTION DID SHE HAVE?
I UNDERSTAND HER SECURITY PEOPLE WANTED TO REMOVE THE SIKHS FROM HER PROTECTIVE DETAIL. SHE STOPPED THEM. SHE SAID, 'AREN'T WE SECULAR?'.
NOW KASHMIR WILL GO UP IN FLAMES. WHY ON EARTH DID SHE GET THAT GUL SHAH TO REPLACE FAROOQ ABDULLAH IN KASHMIR?
THEY SAY HE IS CLOSE TO THE SEPARATISTS.
I THOUGHT THE NELLIE MASSACRE WAS THE WORST THING TO HAPPEN. BUT NOW, AFTER THIS, I DON'T KNOW WHAT WILL HAPPEN NEXT...
RUBBISH!
THERE'S A REAL THREAT TO HER LIFE. THEY SAY THE GRANDKIDS HAVE BEEN BROUGHT BACK FROM DOON AND WELHAM.
THE HINDUSTAN T
CURFEW LIFTED IN CHANDIGAR
DTC BUSES DAMAGED NEAR BANGLA SAHIB

SIX MONTHS BEFORE OPERATION BLUESTAR, AS TROUBLES ESCALATE, MRS GANDHI DECIDES, ON A WHIM, TO FULFIL ONE OF HER LONG-STANDING DESIRES. EVEN THOUGH SHE HAS SPENT A WHOLE DECADE ON PROJECT TIGER, PROTECTING THE MAGNIFICENT NATIONAL ANIMAL, SHE HAS RARELY HAD TIME TO VISIT ANY OF THE NATIONAL PARKS. ONE DAY, SUDDENLY, SHE ARRIVES IN KANHA.
LUCK IS ON HER SIDE.
THROUGH THE GRIM DAYS AND MONTHS THAT ARE TO FOLLOW THIS REMARKABLE EXPEDITION, THE TIGER REMAINS ETCHED IN MRS GANDHI'S MIND. SHE ONLY HAS TO SHUT HER EYES, TO BE TRANSPORTED TO THAT MOMENT, WITH ITS POWERFUL SILENCE, BROKEN ONLY BY THE HUM OF THE FOREST AND THE SOUND OF HER OWN BEATING HEART. EVERY TIME DOUBTS OR SORROWS ASSAIL HER, SHE REMEMBERS THE FOREST AND THE TIGER FROM THAT JANUARY NOON, THE SUN-DAPPLED GRASS AND THE SKY, AND TELLS HERSELF THAT THOUGH SOME THINGS HAVE BEEN LOST, MUCH HAS BEEN FOUND AND PRESERVED TOO.

9

IN WHICH WE LEARN ABOUT ENDINGS

It was the middle of July. Outside, rain clattered down on every surface. Indira was tucked into her bed, a day after the wire had been successfully inserted, connecting her beleaguered heart to the kidneys so blood could flow easier.

'When the heart is enlarged, as in her case, its pumping capacity drops. That's why we had to insert the wire,' the doctor had explained to Miss Das and Rehaan, while Arati and Piya hovered anxiously. 'We were managing it conservatively all this while, but surgery has now become essential.'

For a person who'd had a bunch of tubes put in and taken out several times a day over the last few days, Indira was in surprisingly good humour. For one, Miss Das had taken up the Vanar Sena's cause with immense vigour and had already collected 145 books for the children's library. For another, Piya didi had been her most consistent visitor. While Arati stayed the night, Piya didi stayed with her through the day, sketching and talking (she hadn't yet allowed Piya didi to sketch any of the others in the ward, though she knew Piya didi was itching to draw and the other patients were itching to be drawn).

'Why didn't you ever tell me about the heart treatment?' Piya didi asked when the howling rain gave them some privacy in the ward. The nurses were away at their station; the other patients were all listening to music on their mobile phones. Their relatives were snoozing on the chairs beside them.

'I don't like to tell anyone about it. They would just mollycoddle me unnecessarily. Miss knew, and she worried for me so much in Allahabad. Didn't let me walk around Chowk Mirganj with you... Plus, I don't know, I feel people will say I can't do this or I can't do that because of my heart.'

'Hmm. You know something about Indira Gandhi? When she was your age, people kept saying she was too thin and sickly. Because Kamala Nehru suffered from a young age, Nehru himself—as well as other well-wishers—all believed that Indu had a mysterious "shadow" on her lungs. She spent nine months in a sanatorium in Switzerland—it interrupted her college education. Before she was elected leader by the Congress in 1966, her aunt Vijaylakshmi Pandit issued a barbed statement of support: "Mrs Gandhi has the qualities, now she needs the experience.... She is in very frail health, but with the help of her colleagues, she will manage." That word "frail" stuck for a while. Yet, the more time that passed with her doing the job she loved, the stronger she became. She worked sixteen hours a day as prime minister, and during elections or crises, even longer!'

'She did yoga and exercises, no?'

'She did yoga every morning. And she said in an interview that she "collected" exercises and tried them out when she could. She collected recipes too—but those remained untried.'

'Like you collect recipes,' Indira laughed.

Piya didi rolled her eyes. Her massive collection of cookbooks was a source of mirth for everyone since she loved reading them and spent a large part of her pitiful income buying them—though nobody could ever accuse her of cooking from them.

'I'm sorry I didn't tell you why I was going away,' Piya didi finally said.

'To draw in peace and quiet?'

'Well, yes.'

'To run away from M?' Indira giggled. M had sent a basket with twenty brand new books for the library.

'That too,' said Piya didi. 'You see, sometimes I get really depressed. Not just feeling blue and crying a bit over sad books—I enter this blackness...when I can't possibly believe this feeling will ever end... It's difficult to explain.'

Indira listened carefully. Then she reached out and covered Piya didi's hand with hers. 'My Baba had that too. Same thing. He would be fine, fine, fine. Then, suddenly, it would become dark in his head. Like the bijli had gone and there was a power cut. He couldn't help it. He would drink to forget it. My Dadaji hated it, the drinking, the darkness. But Ma says Baba was very brave, he was never afraid of dying.'

The two of them waited in silence, together, until the feeling that something would happen, just now, went away. 'This time, towards the end, I began to ask myself what would Mrs Gandhi do... You know, she had such busy days, so many responsibilities, but she still had time to worry about the tigers who were being poached and the jharokhas that were being smuggled from Jaisalmer.'

Indira pulled her blanket up. The air-conditioned ward was so cold that Piya brought a little cardigan with her every day. 'Finish the book, please, Piya didi,' Indira said and closed her eyes. 'I want to read it properly.' The soft sound of pencil scratching on paper comforted her. Outside, the rain became thicker and softer, like a grey wool blanket.

Indira slept. Piya felt a rush of happiness as her synapses made a few sudden, luminous leaps in her head. The book would now get done.

Everyone knew how Mrs Gandhi's life had been cut short. But only Piya knew how her story would end.

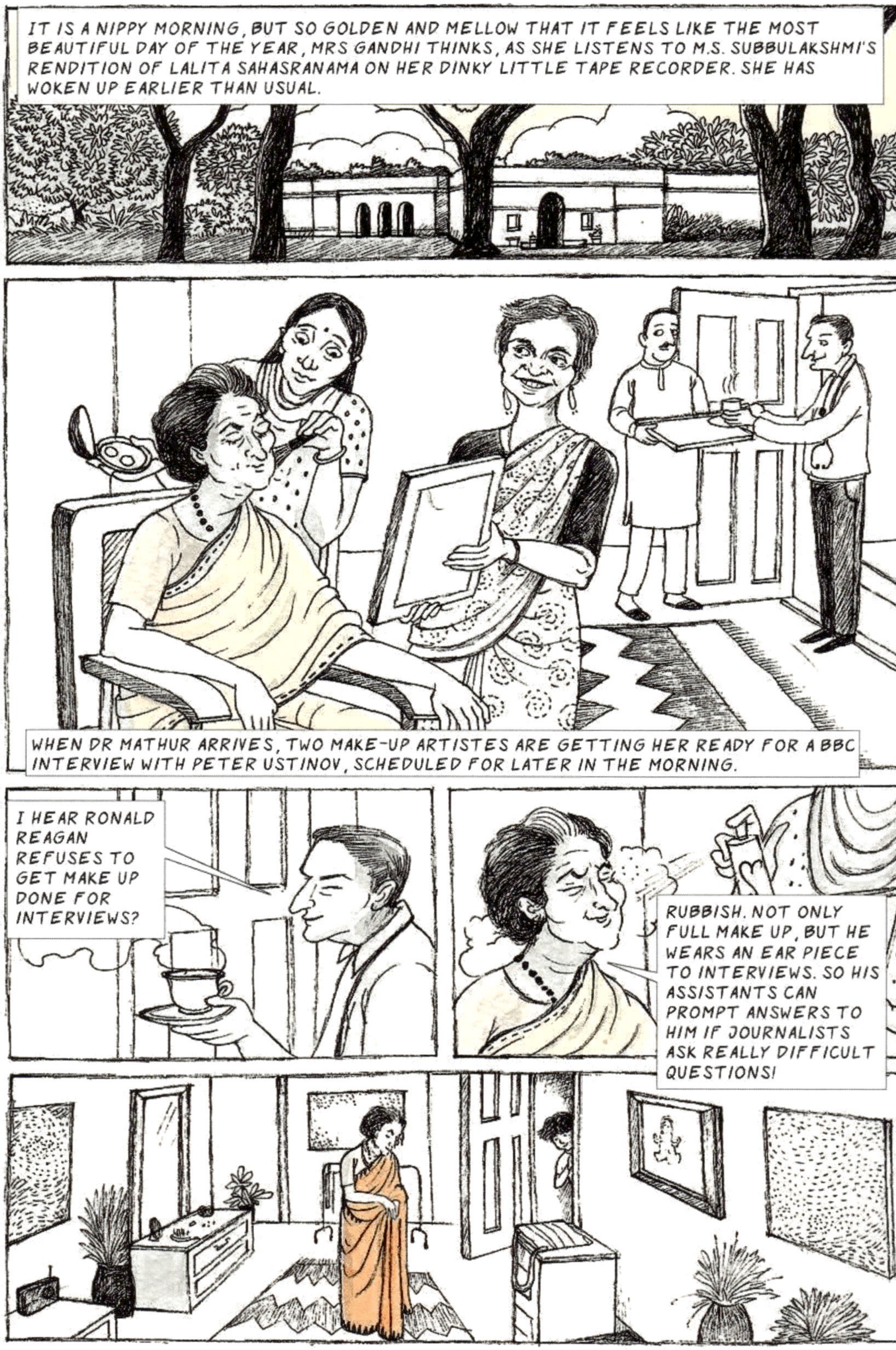
IT IS A NIPPY MORNING, BUT SO GOLDEN AND MELLOW THAT IT FEELS LIKE THE MOST BEAUTIFUL DAY OF THE YEAR, MRS GANDHI THINKS, AS SHE LISTENS TO M.S. SUBBULAKSHMI'S RENDITION OF LALITA SAHASRANAMA ON HER DINKY LITTLE TAPE RECORDER. SHE HAS WOKEN UP EARLIER THAN USUAL.
WHEN DR MATHUR ARRIVES, TWO MAKE-UP ARTISTES ARE GETTING HER READY FOR A BBC INTERVIEW WITH PETER USTINOV, SCHEDULED FOR LATER IN THE MORNING.
I HEAR RONALD REAGAN REFUSES TO GET MAKE UP DONE FOR INTERVIEWS?
RUBBISH. NOT ONLY FULL MAKE UP, BUT HE WEARS AN EAR PIECE TO INTERVIEWS. SO HIS ASSISTANTS CAN PROMPT ANSWERS TO HIM IF JOURNALISTS ASK REALLY DIFFICULT QUESTIONS!

GOOD MORNING, DADI. I AM THE NIRMA BOY IN SCHOOL TODAY.
AH! YOUR KURTA IS DAZZLING WHITE INDEED.
MAY I BORROW YOUR JHOLA?
OH WELL. OKAY. YOU BETTER EMPTY IT THEN.
THANK YOU, DADI.
NATHU RAM, REMEMBER TO BRING IT BACK.

MEANWHILE, ON THE WAY TO SCHOOL...
YOU KNOW SOMETHING ODD? DADI TOLD ME BEFORE LEAVING THAT IF ANYTHING HAPPENS, I SHOULD BE BRAVE...
SHE TOLD ME I AM A DAZZLING NIRMA BOY.
AT 9:10 AM, MRS GANDHI STEPS OUT OF THE WICKET GATE SEPARATING 1 SAFDARJUNG ROAD FROM HER OFFICE ON 1 AKBAR ROAD.

AT 1 SAFDARJUNG ROAD, THE CHILDREN FIND THEIR PARENTS MISSING. FAMILY-FRIENDS FUSS OVER THEM. BUT EVERYTHING IS ASKEW; THE WHOLE HOUSE SEEMS TO TILT DANGEROUSLY.

IN THE AFTERNOON, P WANDERS ABOUT. THERE IS BLOOD ON THE ROAD BETWEEN THE TWO HOUSES AND BULLET CASINGS. IN THE LITTLE SHED AT THE BACK, THERE IS BLOOD ON THE FLOOR.
LATER, SHE WILL LEARN, THIS IS WHERE BEANT SINGH WAS SHOT DEAD BY THE INDO-TIBETAN BORDER POLICE, AGAINST ALL LOGIC, AND SATWANT SINGH WAS GRIEVOUSLY INJURED. AS A RESULT, THE FULL DIMENSIONS OF THE CONSPIRACY AGAINST THE PRIME MINISTER WILL NEVER BE COMPLETELY REVEALED.
LOOKING DOWN FROM HER SECRET PERCH, P REMEMBERS A DIFFERENT TIME, WHEN THEY ALL LIVED TOGETHER.
THEN, AT SOME POINT, HER BROTHER COMES LOOKING FOR HER.

DADI'S STEP IS LIGHT ON THE GRASS AND HER EYES TWINKLE MERRILY. IT IS ALMOST AS IF SHE CAN FLY, BUT CHOOSES NOT TO.

IN WHICH WE EXPRESS GRATITUDE

We are grateful to V.K. Karthika for making our match, leading us into the magnificent world of Mrs G., and then allowing us to experiment hugely with form and structure, without letting the panic register on her face (at least most of the time). Many thanks are due to Vishwajyoti Ghosh for entering the madness at just the right time, and to Shrutika Mathur and Debasri Rakshit for going over the proofs with a fine-toothed sword.

Our families have stood by us through the last year and a half, without asking if the book was ever going to be done. (At least most of the time they didn't ask. Not even when day after day our conversations with them were five words, 'Working on the book. Bye.') So thank you Liza Kuriyan, Jacob Kuriyan (especially, for the anecdotes on the Bangladesh War), Sneha Kuriyan and Sanjeev Cherian, Manidipa Roy, Nilanjan Roy (especially for the anecdotes from the JP movement days in Bihar), Sukumar Jha, Susnato Roy, Saksham and Meenakshi Jha. Also, hat tip to all our friends, who complained incessantly that they have forgotten what we look like. The inimitable Preeti Sahai provided many laughs during expeditions that invariably ended in cold coffee. Much gratitude is due to Shweta and Sibanand Bhol, who provided Priya a home (and a Mac) in Delhi, along with copious quantities of wine. For helping D in a hundred intangible ways, Nayantara and Gitanjali Chatterjee, Chandrashekhar Bhattachayya, Manaspratim Mitra, Arhaan Babar-Ray, the Majumdar-Chakravartys of B-8/4—Subhasree, Saikat, Inaya and Neer—and Sharmistha and Rishi Pratim Mukherjee. Rupa Thapa, for her extraordinary mutton curry, and Madhabi Haldar, for her surreal conversations.

Our warmest acknowledgements are due to Mrs Sonia Gandhi, who offered us the treasures of the library at the Indira Gandhi Memorial Trust to mine and suggested various books that might be useful; she also clarified a few points about Indira Gandhi's Vanar Sena days in Allahabad. Many thanks are due to Mr Jairam Ramesh, who patiently answered questions about P.N. Haksar, the subject of his next book.

At Indira Gandhi Memorial Trust (IGMT), Jaideep Thakur provided the sort of assistance that writers can only dream of; at Nehru Memorial Museum and Library, Dr Ravi K. Mishra not only provided his historian's perspective but also ample samosas and tea. We are grateful to Dinesh Rawat and Rajbir Singh at Parliament House; Dharmendra Tiwari at Swaraj Bhawan; Dr Ravi Kiran and Mohammad Khalid at Anand Bhawan, who ferreted out, upon our request, Nehru's handwritten invitation that he sent out for Indira and Feroze's wedding. Also at Allahabad, the Upadhyayas of Allapur for showing us around the city and Ivan and Purnima Lamech of the charming Kanchan Villa, who led us to Mrs Liddle on Bank Road and provided wonderful meals at the end of long days.

Saurav Jha, our in-house geopolitics and defence expert, helped us understand the world Mrs Gandhi was dealing with and her genius in navigating its many disparate pulls and pressures. He introduced us to Dr V.K. Saraswat, the former head of DRDO, who shared the fascinating story of how the Integrated Guided Missile Development Programme (IGMDP) was sanctioned by Mrs Gandhi, who was, among a hundred other things, an inveterate supporter of the indigenisation of India's military hardware.

Many biographers have dedicated years of their life to Mrs Gandhi. While the biographies by Katherine Frank, Pupul Jayakar and Inder Malhotra became her ready reckoners and lived on her bedside table for the duration of the research, D would also like to record her appreciation for the lesser-known biographies written by K.A. Abbas, with its jaunty energy; the one by Dom Moraes, which, despite its flaws, has the delicious eccentricity of a poet's gaze; and the recent book by Dr K.P. Mathur, Mrs Gandhi's physician, which gave us a few delightful references. Jairam Ramesh's extraordinary biography was published at just the right time to give us the tiger moment, and Sriram Raghavan's meticulously researched book on Bangladesh helped clarify the complicated timelines of 1970-71, though, owing to the nature of the book, we had to simplify things far more than we would have liked to. Finally, we had wanted to situate this book at the intersection of oral history and biography. For that, we must acknowledge everyone who shared their stories, sometimes anonymously. Thank you, Sardar Pal Singh, for your story and for accompanying us on most of our research trips in Delhi. Various originals have inspired the characters. Thank you to Sonia Thapa, who is not Indira, of course, but somewhat Indira-ish; Paras Thapa, who is not Happy but Happy-ish. Miss Reema Das is a tribute to Shreemayee 'Weepli' Das. Weepli shared her students' essays and dramas with D, on demand. A million thanks to Brig. Zubin Minwalla for Dhol Bahadur Thapa's story.

And, finally, we would like to record Priyanka Gandhi Vadra's extraordinary generosity in sharing memories of her Dadi, several of which have made their way into the book.

PRIYA KURIYAN
DEVAPRIYA ROY

A NOTE ON THE TEXT

To arrive at a fresh angle on the life and times of Mrs Gandhi, we had to hunt far and wide for nuggets of information, and it is impossible to provide an exhaustive bibliography. In the interest of maintaining the flow of the narrative, we did not provide footnotes to indicate sources within chapters. However, where Mrs Gandhi addresses the Parliament during the Bangladesh war or the Indian people during the Emergency announcement, we have often quoted directly from her speeches. The same is true of George Fernandes's speech during the Railway Strike, JP's speech in the Emergency section (where he quotes Ramdhari Singh 'Dinkar') and Atal Behari Vajpayee's speech at Ram Lila Maidan. Nixon's comments about India and Mrs Gandhi might seem fictionalized for affect but are, in fact, based on declassified files that are now available in the public domain, though the placement of the comments is naturally imagined. Mrs Gandhi's comment about Chadrashekhar Azad's death is from an interview to Dom Moraes, and several episodes from her childhood and youth are based on her own memories as they appear in the charming little book, *My Truth*. The anecdote about the 1983 World Cup records a conversation between Brian Johnston and Farokh Engineer. The anecdote about the sanctioning of the IGMDP is borrowed from a forthcoming book on India's missile program by V.K. Saraswat and Saurav Jha.

Primary Sources and Biographies

Abbas, K.A. *Indira Gandhi: Return of the Red Rose*. New Delhi: Orient Paperbacks, 1966.
______ *Indira Gandhi: The Last Post*. Bombay: Popular Prakashan, 1985.
______ *That Woman: Her Seven Years in Power*. New Delhi: Indian Book Company, 1973.
Carras, Mary C. *Indira Gandhi: In the Crucible of Leadership*. Boston: Beacon Press, 1979.
Frank, Katherine. *Indira: The Life of Indira Nehru Gandhi* (2001). London: HarperCollins, 2014.
Gandhi, Indira. *Anand Bhawan Memories and Other Personal Essays*. New Delhi: IGMT, 1989.
Gandhi, Indira. *My Truth* (Presented by Emmanuel Pouchpadass). New Delhi: Vision Books, 1980.
Gandhi, Indira. *Remembered Moments: Some Autobiographical Writings*. New Delhi: IGMT, 1987.
Gandhi, Sonia. Ed. *Freedom's Daughter: Letters between Indira Gandhi and Jawaharlal Nehru* (1922-1939). London: Hodder and Stoughton, 1989.
______.Ed. *Two Alone, Two Together: Letters between Indira Gandhi and Jawaharlal Nehru* (1940-1964). London: Hodder and Stoughton, 1992.
Hutheesingh, Krishna Nehru. *Dear to Behold: An Intimate Portrait of Indira Gandhi*. London: Macmillan, 1969.
Jayakar, Pupul. *Indira Gandhi* (1992). New Delhi: Penguin Books, 1995.

Malhotra, Inder. *Indira Gandhi: A Personal and Political Biography*. New Delhi: Hay House, 2014.
Masani, Zareer. *Indira Gandhi*. London: Hamish Hamilton, 1975.
Mathur, K.P. *The Unseen Indira Gandhi: Through Her Physician's Eyes*. New Delhi: Konark, 2016.
Moraes, Dom. *Mrs Gandhi*. London: Jonathan Cape, 1980.
Nehru, Jawaharlal. *An Autobiography* (1936). New Delhi: Penguin Random House India, 2016.
______. *Letters from a Father to a Daughter* (1929). New Delhi: Penguin, 2016.
Prasad, H.Y. Sharada. *Indira Gandhi: A Pictorial Biography* (1986). New Delhi: Puffin Books, 2013.
Ramesh, Jairam. *Indira Gandhi: A Life in Nature*. New Delhi: Simon & Schuster, 2017.
Sahgal, Nayantara. *Indira Gandhi: Tryst with Power* (1982). New Delhi: Penguin, 2012.

Select References

Alexander, P.C. *My Years with Mrs Gandhi*. New Delhi: Vision, 1991.
Bachchan, Harivansh Rai. *In the Afternoon of Time*. (Trans. Dr Rupert Snell). New Delhi: Penguin Random House, 2017.
Baker, Deborah. *A Blue Hand: Allen Ginsberg and the Beats in India*. New Delhi: Penguin, 2011.
Bhushan, Prashant. *The Case that Shook India*. New Delhi: Penguin Random House, 2017.
Bose, Nemai Sadhan. *Indira Gandhi on Herself and Her Times: Her Last and Only Autobiographical Interview*. Calcutta: Ananda Publishers Pvt. Ltd., 1987.
Chatwin, Bruce. 'On the Road with Mrs G.' *What Am I Doing Here*. London: Vintage, 2005.
Dhar, P.N. *Indira Gandhi, the 'Emergency' and Indian Democracy*. New Delhi: OUP, 2001.
Falk, Bertil. *Feroze: the Forgotten Gandhi*. New Delhi: Roli, 2016.
Fotedar, M.L. *Chinar Leaves*. New Delhi: HarperCollins, 2015.
Friedan, Betty. 'Madame Prime Minister.' *'It Changed My Life': Writings on the Women's Movement*. Cambridge: Harvard University Press, 1998.
Hasan, Mushirul. *The Nehrus: Personal Histories*. New Delhi: Lustre Press, 2006.
Hicks, Pamela. *Daughter of Empire: Life As a Mountbatten*. London: Orion, 2013.
Jacob, Lt Gen JFR. *Surrender at Dhaka: Birth of a Nation*. New Delhi: Manohar, 1997.
Kapoor, Coomi. *The Emergency: a Personal History*. New Delhi: Penguin Random House, 2016.
Mehta, Vinod. *The Sanjay Story* (1978). New Delhi: HarperCollins, 2015.
Moraes, Dom. *The Tempest Within: An Account of East Pakistan*. New Delhi: Vikas, 1971.
Mukherjee, Pranab. The Dramatic Decade: The Indira Gandhi Years. New Delhi: Rupa, 2015.
Mukherjee, Rudrangshu. *Nehru and Bose: Parallel Lives*. New Delhi: Penguin, 2015.
Nair, K. Sankaran. *Inside IB and Raw*. New Delhi: Manas, 2008.
Narayan, Jayaprakash. *Prison Diary: 1975*. Bombay: Popular Prakashan, 1977.
Nayar, Kuldeep. *Scoop!: Inside Stories from the Partition to the Present*. New Delhi: HarperCollins, 2006.
Nehru, B.K. *Nice Guys Finish Second* (1997). New Delhi: Penguin Books, 2012.
Prasad, Sharada H.Y. *The Book I Won't be Writing & Other Essays*. Kottayam: DC Publishers, 2003.
Raghavan, Srinath. *1971: A Global History of the Creation of Bangladesh*. New Delhi: Permanent Black, 2015.
Raman, B. *The Kaoboys of RAW*. New Delhi: Lancer, 2009.
Rao Jr., Parsa Venkateshwar. *The Emergency: An Unpopular History*. New Delhi: Har Anand, 2016.
Sahgal, Nayantara. *Prison and Chocolate Cake* (1954). New Delhi: Harper Perennial, 2007.
Schanberg, Sydney. *Beyond the Killing Fields: War Writings*. Lincoln: Potomac Books Inc., 2010.
Seton, Marie. *Panditji: A Portrait of Jawaharlal Nehru*. London: Dobson, 1967.
Shourie, Arun, Prannoy Roy, Rahul Bedi and Shekhar Gupta. *The Assassination and After*. New Delhi: Roli, 1985.
Singh, Tavleen. *Durbar*. New Delhi: Hachette, 2013.
Subramaniam, Arjun. *India's Wars: A Military History, 1947-1971*. New Delhi: HarperCollins, 2016.
Tharoor, Shashi. *Nehru: The Invention of India*. New Delhi: Penguin Books, 2012.
______. *An Era of Darkness: The British Empire of India*. New Delhi: Aleph Book Company, 2016.
Tripathi, Salil. *The Colonel Who Would Not Repent: The Bangladesh War and its Unquiet Legacy*. New Delhi: Aleph Book Company, 2014.
Tully, Mark and Satish Jacob. *Amritsar: Mrs Gandhi's Last Battle*. New Delhi: Rupa, 2006.